Create in Me

Exploring the Pattern of God's Creative Process

Aaron Dailey

renownpublishing

Renown Publishing
www.renownpublishing.com

Create in Me / Aaron Dailey
ISBN-13: 978-1-952602-04-7

A desire that is common to all of humanity is to witness transformation in the self. *Create in Me* displays the mystery and power of God's work of creation and the re-creation of the human heart.

Tyler Johnson | Lead Pastor, Redemption Church, AZ

After reading *Create in Me*, you will never read, study or reflect on the creation narrative the same way. Aaron Dailey presents the secret sauce of God's intent to grow us into balanced disciples who trust Christ. We don't need to strive, hustle, beg, or push for what God has already intended to bestow in us and through us for His glory. This is a recommended work for every believer desiring to dive deeper in call and ministry.

Dr. Michael Carrion | Regional Director, National Latino Evangelical Coalition, VP Church Planting & LD Redeemer City to City

Humanity's struggle has always been to strive for acceptance and approval. In my brother's book, *Create in Me*, you will discover the struggle is over! No longer are you distant and dirty—you have been made clean and brought close.

Ben Dailey | Lead Pastor, Calvary Church, Irving, TX

Through biblical insight, reflective questions, and powerful storytelling, *Create in Me* offers space for the Holy Spirit to do the title of this work in the heart of the reader.

John DelHousaye, PhD | Professor of New Testament and Spiritual Formation, Phoenix Seminary

I appreciate Aaron's passion to see both individuals and communities fully encounter the Spirit of God and to be freed from the lies that hold us in bondage and transform us to a new creation. *Create in Me* is a work birthed from Aaron's passion for God and love for those he serves, and I recommend this work!

Dennae Pierre | Executive Director, Surge Network

Your journey of transformation needs a guide like Aaron Dailey. In this book, you will find that Aaron is a pastor who has shaped his entire ministry around a core belief that the Spirit works in transformative ways to create and re-create people and communities. He writes from a life of lived convictions and experience. Prepare to be guided and loved well by him as you read this book.

Vermon Pierre | Lead Pastor of Roosevelt Community Church, Phoenix, AZ

I have come to appreciate Aaron as a dear brother who has been formed by his openness and insight into Scripture. This book gives some insight into the process of how he has become more rooted in the gospel. I heartily recommend listening to him!

Dr. Michael W. Goheen | Author, *Drama of Scripture: Finding Our Place in the Biblical Story*

This book and journal is so encouraging. To be brought into God's creative process, and see how He is still creating in me through the same process He created the universe, has stirred something in me. Aaron not only draws our attention to that process but also invites us to sync up with that same process of creativity as we engage the book. A true gem and breath of fresh air.

Wayne Wynter | Lead Pastor, Redemption Alhambra Church, Phoenix, AZ

*It's impossible to thank everyone, but I must dedicate this
book to both my biological family and my church family.*

*Dana, I'm the lucky one. You inspired and
lived this book with me—we wrote this.*

*My beloved children, you are a constant reminder of grace
and of our Father giving good gifts.
Your dad loves you deeply!*

*Mom and Dad, you taught me to hear God's voice, which enabled me to
recognize when He was whispering this book into my ear.*

*Dailey brothers, your fingerprints are all over this book.
Thanks for being not only good brothers but also good friends.*

*Tez, your generosity, push, and friendship helped birth this book.
You are the midwife of this project.*

*Redemption Church (pastors, leaders, family), God has given me a heart for
you, and you have my heart. Thanks for giving me a place on this earth that
feels like home and gives me glimpses of heaven.*

CONTENTS

God's Creative Process

This book is deeply personal. As you flip through its pages, you will be reading my prayer journal, full of meditations born out of my desperate need for God. This is not me putting my best foot forward. It's me coming as I am and sharing from my heart the abundance of grace God has poured out on me. I feel insecure and vulnerable sharing a message that was a personal, edifying revelation for me. I did not initially write it with the intention that others would read it, that others would get a glimpse into this intimate exchange with God. The pages that follow paint a picture of my relationship with Jesus and His work of spiritual formation in me.

I used to think that I had this walk-with-Jesus life figured out. So how did I get to the place where I found myself crying out to God for intervention? It didn't come easily.

I grew up as a pastor's kid and thought that I knew everything. I was in leadership positions in every club and ministry since early high school. I officially worked in church ministry since I was 18 and planted a church at the age of 24.

I was a "good boy" who felt like I was morally better than everyone else, and I preached a self-righteous message. I was trying to earn favor from God and ultimately trying to *make myself* into who I wanted to be. I was on the hunt for success but called it purpose. I was blinded by pride and was trying to use God as a means to reach my dreams. The gospel I heard and preached was not good news at all! It was a message of condemnation, morality, and success. I felt like I had to climb a ladder in my own strength to get to God, and I always fell far short.

After years of striving, I hit a wall. I couldn't do it anymore. There was no strength left in me to keep climbing. Everything I thought I knew was meaningless. I felt so lost.

In that place, all around and within me was darkness, "formless and empty" (Genesis 1:2). I had come to the end of myself. All of my attempts to prove myself, all of my striving to reach God, fell short. I tried to earn favor from God and make myself into someone I wanted to be, and I failed. I sought out purpose and success, using God as my means to get there, and I didn't find it. I became aware of the darkness I was in and could see my sin and self-righteousness at war with God. I felt the void all humanity feels. In the same moment, I realized that I didn't know how to fix or rebuild my brokenness.

In that place, God *came to me*. He met me where I was, right in the middle of my brokenness. Through His Word, He shone a light into my darkness and changed everything for me. I know that it sounds too simple, but three words became a miraculous, God-inspired revelation that the Holy Spirit used to jump-start His spiritual formation in my life. These three words were breathed by God and penned by a man who was well acquainted with this dark place in which I found myself.

Create in me....

In that moment, reading Psalm 51, I was brought to the end of all my striving. A prayer filled my heart and echoed the psalm of David: "Create in me..., O God" (Psalm 51:10). I had read this verse before, but this time it was no longer just a song of David, but also the melody of my own heart. My voice lifted in harmony with David, asking for mercy, compassion, and cleansing.

Those three words spurred a thought that sent me into years of meditation and prayer. I realized that the God who created the world was the same God whom David was asking to create a clean heart within him. I asked God, "Lord, if you can create the whole world, can you do that work of creation in me?"

I began to see God as an artist with a creative process. When He created the world, He didn't bring it all into existence in a single, big-bang moment. Genesis 1 reveals that God had an intentional *process* for creating the world. It took time, and there was a pattern to His work of creation. It made me wonder if God's process for creation could be seen in other aspects of biblical history, in the church, and in me. What I discovered completely revolutionized the way I look at the Christian life. The same God who created the whole world is still creating.

This book is the fruit of those years of prayer, study, and pastoral ministry. It is the unfolding of everything God revealed to me about His creative process as He creates us in His image daily. In the pages ahead, we'll look at God's intentional process in Genesis 1 and observe how He is still creating in this beautiful pattern. We will look at examples from the Bible, and we'll see that pattern unfold again and again.

I don't think my story is that unique. I think everyone can relate to this place in life. Feelings of darkness, emptiness, and hopelessness are common threads that tie humanity together. I have had the privilege of pastoring for many years, and people let me in on their stories.

I will share my story and the stories of others because I want you to know that you're not alone, that *all* of us are in process. We all start in a place of darkness, needing God to begin His creative work in us. In addition to my own story, I will share stories throughout this book inspired by people in my own life who have found themselves in dark places, searching for purpose and meaning (names have been changed for privacy).

We are not unique in feeling like we are in the dark and cannot see the light. We are not alone when we sit in that place, formless, void, and empty. We are not alone in our desire to have a full life.

If you're coming to this book from a place of brokenness— like the place where I found myself—I offer you this beacon of hope: though your life feels bleak and dark right now, you are in a better place than you think. Though you feel far from the finish line, take heart because you are in the perfect place for God to move.

The God who spoke the whole universe into existence from nothing and created order from chaos is the same God who can and will speak directly into the chaos of your life and transform it into a life filled with purpose.

I have created a "Workbook Journal" at the end of each chapter for you. These journal sections exist as a space for you to lean into your Creator. When you come before God through these sections, just be yourself. You have the freedom to make notes, draw pictures, write out prayers, or anything else you'd like. I encourage you to consider using these prompts in a separate notebook or journal so that you have as much space as you need. Be creative. Make memories. Most importantly, use these prompts to help you grow, learn, and spend time with Jesus.

This book is meant to be a sign pointing you to the God who does the work of new creation. I know that you want to change quickly, but let me encourage you to slow down. Instead of trying to work harder and make something happen, put yourself in a posture of listening and waiting. You will discover your created purpose as you seek to know and abide in your Creator. You can rest, knowing that the God who started this creative work in you will bring it to completion (Philippians 1:6). I am confident that God will use this book to speak to you and do His work in and through you.

Introduction Prompts

The same God who created the world
is still creating in me.

Meditate on these Scripture verses: Genesis 1:1; Psalm 51;
Colossians 1:15–16; Isaiah 43:1–7.

Ponder:

* The God of all creation is the same God who will create in you.

* Take a few moments and think about God being eternal. Then draw or write down your thoughts about the greatness of God.

_____

_____

_____

_____

_____

_____

_____

_____

_____

_____

_____

_____

_____

Questions: How would you describe how you feel in your life right now? What have you been asking God to do for you?

_____

_____

_____

_____

_____

_____

_____

_____

_____

_____

_____

_____

Prayer: Spend time reading Psalm 51. Then journal your own prayer of repentance.

_____

_____

_____

_____

_____

_____

_____

_____

_____

_____

_____

_____

Activity: On a separate piece of paper, write out your dreams—anything you dream of doing, becoming, having, or owning. Then, as an act of faith, destroy the piece of paper to symbolize that you are surrendering your dreams to Jesus in exchange for His plans for your life. This will feel uncomfortable, but it is a meaningful symbol of dying to self and asking God to resurrect only what is of Him.

Introduction | *Thoughts and Drawings*

Let There Be Light

And God said, "Let there be light," and there was light. God saw that the light was good, and he separated the light from the darkness.
—Genesis 1:3–4

In him was life, and that life was the light of all mankind. The light shines in the darkness, and the darkness has not overcome it. ... The true light that gives light to everyone was coming into the world.
—John 1:4–5, 9

A good movie takes you out of this world and into a new one. It helps you to escape your realities and to forget for just a moment about the struggles of this life.

My wife of over twenty years, Dana, and I love to watch movies together. No matter the movie's quality, we love the opportunity to check out of reality, check into another world, and be entertained by someone else's story. Sometimes we have so much fun in that created world that we are reluctant to return to the real world and its struggles.

One of the most crucial scenes of any film is its opening. Those first twenty minutes set the stage for everything that leads us to the final conflict and resolution. In those opening moments, we see what writers call "world building." It's where we, as viewers (or readers), see the unveiling of a world. We're introduced to a little bit of the culture and sometimes to a little bit of backstory for our main characters. Why? So that we, as an audience, can develop a sort of relationship with the characters of the film. After all, why would we care what happens to them if we don't first care about them?

When you begin a relationship with someone, there's not a whole lot you know about that person. You have to spend time talking with, interacting with, and observing the person so you can start to understand his or her patterns and rhythms of life. In time, you learn to appreciate and love the nuances and quirks of his or her personality. As well as you think you are getting to know the person, you always have to leave room for him or her to surprise you.

One of the most surprising things about a relationship, however, isn't what you learn about the other person. It's what you learn about yourself. It's not much different when it comes to your relationship with God.

The truth is that we will never be able to find our created purpose until we find the Creator's purpose. To find the Creator's purpose, we must know God and understand His heart and intention for creating the world in the first place. He wanted to have a relationship with people and to engage in close fellowship and communion with us. This is His heart for us and our primary purpose: that we may know Him and fellowship with Him. To see that, we need only go back to the beginning, back to Genesis.

God the Eternal, Our Creator

In the beginning God created the heavens and the earth.
                                    —*Genesis 1:1*

When it comes to storytelling, it's important to pay attention to the order in which the characters appear. Most of the time, the first character to appear is the hero, sometimes called the protagonist. After that, you'll sometimes find the best friend or gutsy sidekick and, of course, the villain.

This is important to note because the first character on the scene in Genesis isn't Adam, and it's not the devil. It's the Creator, God Himself. In the first two chapters of Genesis, we see the ultimate example of world building. When I looked at the story in that light, it completely changed my perspective on life. Our story isn't about us. It's about the One who created us.

The very first verse of Genesis tells us that before the beginning, before creation, before anything ever existed, God was there. If time had a back door and you opened it to look into history, you would see God. If time had a front door and you could open it into the future, God would be there. God is not boxed into time because He created time.

As hard as is it for us, with our linear thinking, to imagine, God is the only uncreated, perfectly loving, all-powerful, glorious, holy, righteous being ever to exist. But just as we crave companionship with others, so does He. He looked into the darkness, blankness, and nothingness of the unformed world and decided that out of His goodness, He would create something marvelous: the world, us.

We did nothing to earn the favor of existing. It was a gift given to us out of love. Remember the pattern I mentioned earlier in this chapter that we start noticing in relationships? Well, this is one of those things, and it's crucial for us to remember going forward that our eternal God's actions are always based on His love, power, glory, and righteousness. He acts because of who He is, not because of who we are. The creation story and the idea of God creating in us is about God and initiated by God, completely apart from us.

> *It is for freedom that Christ has set us free. Stand firm, then, and do not let yourselves be burdened again by a yoke of slavery.*
> **—Galatians 5:1**

This can be a word of freedom when you are living life for yourself and think that the world revolves around you. Knowing this reoriented my life from being self-focused or purpose-focused to God-focused. I was set free when I realized that I did not do anything to earn God's love and favor. This is all about God. Out of His love, He chose me before the foundations of the world. I was tired from striving for something that I had already been given, and I was set free to receive all Christ had supplied.

"Let There Be Light"

> *Now the earth was formless and empty, darkness was over the surface of the deep, and the Spirit of God was hovering over the waters.*

And God said, "Let there be light," and there was light. God saw
that the light was good, and he separated the light from the darkness.

—Genesis 1:2–4

Now that we've seen who our hero is, we have the opportunity
to get a glimpse at the world in which He operated. Scripture
describes the uncreated earth in three words: "formless," "empty,"
and "dark." Notice in verse 3 that God didn't jump into creating
us after creating the heavens and the earth. If He had, He would
have plunged us into a dark void in which we would have per-
ished immediately.

Instead, God's second act of creation was to separate light
from darkness. Similarly, His first act of new creation in our lives
is to shed a powerful light of truth that exposes darkness for what
it is: an empty void.

For you were once darkness, but now you are light in the Lord. Live
as children of light....

—Ephesians 5:8

I don't believe we have to make that far of a leap to see that
these words also describe the human heart before God speaks
into and creates in our lives. Before we come to Christ, our hearts
are essentially like the unformed earth—without shape, without
purpose, and without the possibility for true life. Apart from God,
we are empty, and no matter how we try to fill the void in our
lives, we are still just as empty as we were before.

To illustrate, consider the stories of Kendrick, Rosa, Carl, and
Hope.

Kendrick wakes up every day before sunup and heads to a low-paying construction job. It is back-breaking work, but what hurts worse than his body is the pain he feels inside from not doing what he loves. Every time he plays the piano, he feels complete and free. But when he wakes up every morning for work, he has to drag himself out of bed. He can't help thinking that he is living in a nightmare and feeling that he was created for more than this.

Rosa's first love was the dream of being a psychologist, and then she met Jose. Love blinded her, and marriage and motherhood were eye-opening experiences. Rosa now feels like she gave up on her career for her husband and children. Home is a prison keeping her locked away from her purpose. She hates kissing Jose goodbye as he runs off to work to chase his dreams, because she feels like she's kissing her own dreams goodbye. She's irritated, empty, and cold in all of her relationships. Her faith in God is nonexistent because she feels like He is keeping her from her created purpose.

Carl's loneliness has overtaken his life and feels like a disease. He wants a woman so badly that he doesn't even care who she is; he is just tired of being alone. Carl has subscriptions on every dating website. He is in every club, goes to every bar, and attends a church with single women, all in hopes of finding love. He can't talk to a girl without first thinking, "Could she be the one?" He has prayed for years and can't pray anymore because he thinks that God isn't listening. His loneliness often leads him to think of death because that seems better than living alone. He screams at God, "Why have You created me to be alone?"

Hope is convinced that her name is a curse. It seems like a cruel joke to have a name you can never understand. She was abused as a child, and there is no way she could ever dream of feeling hopeful. Her past haunts her every day. The images that pop into her head make her feel crazy. She can't help but yell at the images because they seem so real. To think that there could be a God only makes her angrier. How could a loving God create her and place her in a life of so much pain?

The people in these stories all found themselves sitting in darkness, empty. This is how the world began, and this is where all of our God-stories start, too.

God Calls His Creation into the Light

In the beginning was the Word, and the Word was with God, and the Word was God. He was with God in the beginning. Through him all things were made; without him nothing was made that has been made. In him was life, and that life was the light of all mankind. The light shines in the darkness, and the darkness has not overcome it.

—John 1:1–5

Just as God separated the light and the darkness in Genesis 1, God's light calls us into transparency, honesty, confession, and vulnerability. He calls us to bring all of who we are, including our darkness, before all of who He is, "the light of the world" (John 8:12).

We all know what it means to lie in bed at night, feeling hollow, and to be in darkness, where everything is hidden, because we'd rather run straight into the darkness. We don't want people to see who we really are, and we end up lost, unable to see ourselves or where we are going.

If you're reading this book while in the midst of the darkness, take heart! If we learn anything from Genesis 1:2–3, it's that God, not darkness, has the last word.

When God spoke into the darkness, there was nothing to deserve the power of God's Word. He spoke before anything could ever respond, give back, or even exist. There was nothing to say, "I am just rough around the edges and need a little cleaning up, but I think I would be a good asset to your team."

Trying to find your purpose as God's creation on your own would be like the formless, blank canvas of the world trying to spark a seed of life apart from God's command. It can't be done.

All that was about to be created out of the blankness and blackness came completely from the character, love, beauty, and wonder of the heart of God. In showing us that all things are completely given as gifts of grace, because He is the only one who has enough power and creativity to produce them, God shows us that His Word will never return void or empty (Isaiah 55:11). Just as God didn't leave the earth in darkness but called forth the light, He calls us, as members of His creation, out of the dark and into the light (1 Peter 2:9).

This may seem too easy or miraculous to those who are striving to create themselves, but this is life for those who are weary. We need God to speak His Word! Speak Lord, and we will listen.

Walking in Light

This is the message we have heard from him and declare to you: God is light; in him there is no darkness at all. If we claim to have fellowship with him and yet walk in the darkness, we lie and do not live out the truth. But if we walk in the light, as he is in the light, we have fellowship with one another, and the blood of Jesus, his Son, purifies us from all sin.

—1 John 1:5–7

Many people emphasize the power of God's Word, that He could speak all things into existence, but rarely do we meditate on the graciousness of His Word. But the story of creation shows in a vibrant picture that God does not work in darkness.

Creation serves as evidence of the message John and the other apostles spread throughout the world, a message that continues to be carried forward today. When God created us, He created us with a purpose. When we aren't sure of that purpose or we ignore it because we're too caught up in our own efforts, we flounder through life, wandering in darkness. Our reality becomes a non-reality.

The first words that God spoke declare much about the solid, dependable nature of His character. When we ask God to move and to work in our lives, the first thing He is going to do is break through the darkness and turn on the light of His Word. This means that everything we have hidden will be exposed—not to God, who already sees our brokenness and rebelliousness clear as day, but to ourselves. Sometimes what's revealed to us is more than we feel like we can bear.

Saul, from the book of Acts, is a good example. Before he became Paul, he was in darkness and extremely zealous in per-secuting the Christians, including Stephen (Acts 6–8). Saul was a terrorist by all standards, murdering in the name of God. Like all the others who did not believe Jesus was the Messiah, Saul's mind was blinded to the things of God, and the gospel did not shine through to him. His heart was dark, formless, and void. The only thing that was going to save Saul was an act of God.

God moved while Saul was on the road to Damascus (Acts 9). God broke into the darkness of Saul's heart with a powerful, blinding light and a voice that exposed his sin: "Saul, Saul, why do you persecute me?" (Acts 9:4). The first thing God did in Paul's life was turn on the light and show Paul what he was doing. God revealed Himself to Paul.

There is nothing more exposing, yet covering, than the light of God turning on. In Saul's transformation, the light shone bright on that Damascus road and pierced through the darkness of his heart and mind so powerfully that he believed in the Lord, and God changed his name from Saul to Paul.

In the same way, God begins working in our lives, and that motivates us to move toward Him and the purpose for which He created us. When we pray, "Create in me" (Psalm 51:10), we'd better be ready to escape the darkness forever because God only exists in the light. He *is* light (1 John 1:5).

First John 1:6 speaks to the elements of darkness and light: "If we claim to have fellowship with him and yet walk in the darkness, we lie and do not live out the truth." There is great danger to us, according to John, in walking in duality. Apart from God, it is impossible for us to walk in the light. Even great leaders of the faith, like David, have been brought down by secrets that they kept in the dark in order to keep up appearances, rather than confessing that they were just as broken as the rest of us and in desperate need of God's help (2 Samuel 11–12).

Our greatest freedom comes when we stop trying to hide our brokenness and lie about our sin and instead cry out, "Create in me a pure heart, O God" (Psalm 51:10). The light comes on, and we see fully who we are in the light. We are fully exposed and yet fully covered, just as we see in the first day of creation, the creation of light.

When you recognize that you have been living for your own glory and you run to God, crying out, "Create in me a clean heart," you will realize that everything you have built and strived for is nothing in comparison to what God has planned for you. You will come to the place where you are not asking self-righteous questions, such as "What do I have to do to get back to my created purpose?" or "What do I have to do to fix this situation?"

Instead you will recognize your need to cry out to a gracious and powerful God to speak, move, and create in you because you are empty, lost, formless, and in darkness. Your sin and striving may have gotten you into whatever mess or struggle you're in, but God's Word will move you out of it.

The True Light

Remember Kendrick? He knows that he needs to provide for his kids, but when he drags himself out of bed every morning, he feels a deep sense of dissatisfaction. He wants to do what he was created to do.

He has been chasing music, his passion, thinking that it would be the light for him. His world seems dark because he thinks that he has no real purpose or fulfillment in his job. He wonders if God is near or if He even cares.

The reality is that God is near and He does care. The issue is that music is *not* Kendrick's true light! Music, in and of itself, was never designed to bring fulfillment and give purpose. It is a gift from a creative God. As long as Kendrick is trying to find the light in music, he will only find darkness.

Kendrick needs what we all need: the loving Creator to break in and reveal Himself as the true light. That will free him from chasing created things (Romans 1:25). Then he can see himself and music in the true light of the gospel.

Step One of God's Creative Process: God Reveals the Light

I've mentioned before that when I read Genesis 1, I began to see a pattern in the creative process God uses as He makes us a new creation. On the first day of creation, God said, "Let there be light" (Genesis 1:3). He spoke light into the darkness, the void. And this is His first step when He makes you a new creation. He speaks into your emptiness and says, "Let there be light."

That is the first gospel proclamation. God must speak the Word and reveal to you the light of the gospel in the face of Jesus. Jesus is the light that came into the darkness. Seeing Him and knowing Him is the first step, and He leads you into every other step from that point forward.

The apostle Paul said it this way:

> *Therefore, since through God's mercy we have this ministry, we do not lose heart. Rather, we have renounced secret and shameful ways; we do not use deception, nor do we distort the word of God. On the contrary, by setting forth the truth plainly we commend ourselves to everyone's conscience in the sight of God. And even if our gospel is veiled, it is veiled to those who are perishing. The god of this age has blinded the minds of unbelievers, so that they cannot see the light of the gospel that displays the glory of Christ, who is the image of God. For what we preach is not ourselves, but Jesus Christ as Lord, and ourselves as your servants for Jesus' sake. For God, who said,*

"Let light shine out of darkness," made his light shine in our hearts
to give us the light of the knowledge of God's glory displayed in the
face of Christ.

—2 Corinthians 4:1–6

If you find yourself in a dark place, know this: you are blinded by the god of this age. If you need the start of a new day in your life, I know that Jesus and His mercies are the dawn of that newness. I am praying for you! I am praying that the same Jesus who took me out of darkness and revealed Himself to me will start this work of new creation in you.

This process will not start unless God, who created all things, reveals Himself to you in the person of Jesus. You *need* to know Him! You can't know God unless you know Jesus. You can't know yourself if you don't know Him. You cannot make this happen. The good news is that we serve a God who, since the beginning, has been coming to us. Jesus is the embodiment of light coming to us, and I believe He will do that for you.

This puts you in a great place to cry out in prayer. Like David did and I did, cry out to God because your Father hears and is the only One who is able to start and finish this great work of making you into all He has created you to be.

Stop (I know this is a weird thing for an author to do, but I want you to encounter Jesus more than I want you to finish my book) and spend time asking God to show you who He is in His kindness, His love, and His mercy. Pray that He would break into your life and show you the light in the face of Jesus. Slow down and let Him show you the things that are empty and void. Allow Him to bring them into His light so that you can repent and let God's grace and mercy cover and cleanse you.

If something is starting in you and your affections are being stirred for Jesus, know that God is working in you by His Spirit. This is not the book; this is God working in you! If you feel like I am talking to you and the words on these pages are written just for you, then know that God is speaking to you. Your Father in heaven is pursuing you and opening your eyes. You are receiving a revelation of your need for the light, for Jesus. Trust Him and give your life to Him because the life He has for you cannot be lived apart from a relationship with Him. This is the dawn of the new day you have been praying for.

Chapter One Prompts

You need the light of God to break into your darkness.

Meditate on these Scripture verses: Genesis 1:1–5; 1 John 1:5; John 1:1–4; 2 Corinthians 4:1–6.

Ponder:

* The light is seen in the face of Jesus.

* You need God to turn on the light.

* Think about God creating light before He created the sun. Think about Jesus being the light. Draw or write down your thoughts and the connections you see between these two ideas.

_____

_____

_____

_____

_____

_____

_____

_____

_____

_____

_____

_____

_____

Questions: Why did God turn on the light as His first act of creation? What does the light do that makes you want to stay in the darkness?

_____

_____

_____

_____

_____

_____

_____

_____

_____

_____

_____

_____

Prayer: Journal a prayer of faith that is personal and vulnerable, asking God to turn on the light in your heart. Thank Him that He is not hiding Himself from you but, rather, is opening your eyes to trust in Jesus.

_____

_____

_____

_____

_____

_____

_____

_____

_____

_____

_____

_____

_____

Activity: Set your alarm to wake you early in the morning so you can watch the sunrise. Let God meet you there. Take a journal and write down your prayers to Him. Snap a picture to remember the time of prayer and place it in your book as a reminder of the light of Jesus.

Chapter One | *Thoughts and Drawings*

CHAPTER TWO

Let There Be a Space

Then God said, "Let there be a space between the waters, to separate the waters of the heavens from the waters of the earth."

—Genesis 1:6 (NLT)

And the Word became flesh and dwelt among us, and we have seen his glory, glory as of the only Son from the Father, full of grace and truth.

—John 1:14 (ESV)

Some of the best years of my vocational life were spent developing and running a residential/commercial painting company. It was rewarding work, and the crews of tradespeople I worked with became close friends.

Many people get the sense that trade work is only something you do when you have failed in life and that no one could possibly be passionate about such hard and humble work. Customers often told me that they would paint their houses themselves, but they just didn't have time. In a sense, they thought painting was such a low-skilled job that anyone could do it if he or she just had time.

But in reality, painters are some of the most overlooked and undervalued tradespeople in society. What most people don't know is that about ninety percent of the work a painter does is the *preparation* work before any painting even gets done. The painter has to prepare the surfaces for painting and spends the majority of the time power washing, filling cracks and gaps, scraping off old paint, priming, caulking, sanding, and matching textures.

Customers only see the end results. Because they are not always aware of all the steps it takes, it's easy to think that the painter merely slaps paint on the wall and calls it good, but that is just not true. Only an amateur painter would do it that way. This is why we need painters who have integrity and take pride in their work, because much of what they do goes unrecognized or unappreciated.

Space to Create

For the second day of creation, I want you to think of God as a tradesman doing the work that goes unnoticed and unrecognized. God is unlike any artist I know; He shows us His creative process and doesn't just present the finished product. The second day of creation was the day He prepared *space to create.*

This day went unnoticed by those who watched. It even went unvalidated by God because it was the only day God did not say, "It is good," at the end of it. When I noticed this in my studies, it reminded me of all the work professionals do that goes unnoticed or unvalidated, the work for which no one pats us on the back or says, "Good job," when it's done.

Unlike God, we are prone to doing only the things that get noticed or validated. When that's the case, we miss doing the important work of preparation, thinking that no one will notice. If we are honest, many of the changes that happen physically, habitually, and mentally in our lives happen in the mundane moments. It can be overwhelming to recognize all the unseen things we will have to do, so we don't even start, or we give up when no one notices. This is what happened to me. I felt that I was far from what God wanted of me, and I knew how long it would take to change, so I had no hope that it could be done.

In this chapter, there may be an urge to move to the next steps quickly, but I challenge you to slow down. I don't want you to miss the importance of what God was doing when He said, "Let there be a space" (Genesis 1:6 NLT).

In the Chaos

Sometimes in our lives, we become bored with repetition or mundane practices because these are things we've heard or done before. But what's interesting is that important truths are understood only through repetition and intentional remembrances.

Have you noticed, so far, that each day of creation began with God speaking? Every day of creation was initiated by the voice of God and then followed by obedience to that command. God's

Word is what moves every step of the re-creation of our lives after we come to Christ. This should make us desperate for God to speak into our lives. We live by every Word that proceeds out of His mouth (Matthew 4:4). We need revelation.

In Genesis 1:6–8, on the second day of creation, God spoke into the darkness. He reached into the waters to make space. This space was made to display His light. In this same pattern, God continues to speak into and create in the deepest pockets of your being and your life. This is called *sanctification*. Hear this: God does His work of sanctification not by bringing you out of the disorder or chaos but by making space right in the middle of it.

Without going into a huge theological discussion, sanctification simply is God's ongoing creative process by which believers are set apart for His special use. We are separated unto God's work, whatever He would have for us at whatever stage in our lives. This work of sanctification is started, sustained, and completed by the Word of God.

Intentional Preparation

There is some discussion around what it means when God separated the waters above and the waters below. Some believe it could be a poetic way of describing the clouds, while others take it literally as a pre-flood canopy covering the earth that created a perfect greenhouse effect. However you want to look at it, one thing is undeniable: God made a space—"an expanse" (Genesis 1:6 ESV) or "a vault" (Genesis 1:6) of sky—*among* the unstable waters. He made this space with room for everything He was about to create.

This space was perfectly made and given its form by the Word of God, and His Word was the only barrier holding the waters above from collapsing back into the waters below. It is awe-inspiring to imagine how the order of a perfectly created world was placed among chaos, which only God's Word held at bay.

When you look at the second day of creation, it doesn't seem like God did much. There were no big flashes of light pressing the darkness, there was no surge of waves as land emerged from the deep, and there was no explosion of color as plant life blossomed for the first time. Yet, without the space God created on the second day—this seemingly dull or inconsequential act—life as we know it today could not exist. And so it is with us.

The work of sanctification, or separation, can feel like being in the desert for forty years or in the wilderness for forty days. You wonder, "Did anything productive actually happen in my life over these last days or years?" It seems mundane and normal. You often don't get validation for it, and it can go unnoticed, but it is an extremely important part of God's work of new creation in you.

Being in process can feel like buying a piece of land on which you plan to build a house. You buy the land; it belongs to you. You level the property and do some work, but it is still dirt with nothing visibly beautiful on it.

You know that you belong to God. He has given you a new identity, but did anything actually change visibly? Maybe you can't see it yet, and you feel like you have a long way to go.

The day when God made space is an important reminder for those of us who are in process. God is doing something in you, and you cannot see it yet because the seed is still buried in the ground. You are in a season when God is cleaning things out, making space, and leveling dirt in your life. God is patiently doing prep work, and no one, including yourself, can see the final outcome. This day when God makes space is for you.

God is a God of order. He needs space to work. God saw the darkness and chaos, and He saw everything He could make. He went right in the middle of the darkness and the waters and made a space to create something beautiful and miraculous.

I know this can seem boring, but it's a rich part of God's creative process. When God begins His work of new creation in us, it is easy to wish that He would do His work in an instantaneous, big-bang moment. But God is a master builder; He does things intentionally over time. He didn't make the world in a single, big-bang moment, and He doesn't complete your spiritual formation in an instant. He keeps you in His hands, and He will be faithful to complete what He starts (Philippians 1:6).

Common Grace

It is difficult for us to tell how much grace we are living under. We are unaware of and unthankful for the protection God's Word provides for all of us in common grace. It's like the old Chinese proverb: "If you want to know what water is, don't ask the fish." It's difficult to describe something that is a constant, natural part of your existence. When you haven't experienced anything else, how can you put your reality into words? You can't describe what you take for granted.

We all live under and in God's common grace and protection. Unfortunately, sometimes for us to see the importance of what we take for granted, we have to experience life without God's protection. When we overlook the space of grace, it becomes the space where God disciplines us, always with the intent to draw us back to Himself. He disciplines those He loves (Hebrews 12:6).

In Genesis 6–9, we see the story of Noah and the ark. Sin was judged by God, and He caused the waters above and below to collapse back in on each other, destroying the earth. The protective space God created, a perfect atmosphere, came crashing upon creation during the flood (Genesis 7:11–12). In a moment of time, God removed that protective space to bring discipline and to point creation back to Himself.

We can take the atmosphere we live in for granted because we are always living under this protection. But we must see that if not for the grace and power of God, we all would be crushed by the waters of chaos. We are always living under God's protection, even when we don't notice it.

Sanctified in the Midst of Chaos

After the flood, it was as if life on the earth began again. The remnant from the flood started fresh, with a clean slate. They began again with the work of filling the earth. God seems to continue this pattern of re-creation throughout His story by reaching into the chaos of a sin-diseased world and choosing a people.

God separated Israel for Himself as a chosen people to shine forth His light to the nations. He chose Noah and his family as pictures of His righteousness in the midst of a broken and depraved world. He sent Jesus to make His home among us and sit at tables with sinners.

To sanctify is to set apart or declare holy, to consecrate.[1] God shines His light through a sanctified people living in His favor and protection among the chaos of sin. When He separates for Himself a people, He does not pull them *out* of a sinful world. Rather, He makes a space in the *middle* of the nations to reveal Himself.

Another picture of this space of grace happened when Israel was fleeing Egypt (Exodus 14). As they crossed the Red Sea, the waters were held back. God provided a space of grace to deliver them from Egypt. God held back the waters of the Red Sea and allowed them to cross on dry land. Just like Noah and his family, the Israelites were protected and delivered because of God's favor and choosing. As soon as they crossed, God removed His hand from holding back the waters. The space which gave the Israelites safe passage became the space where God crushed their enemies.

God worked the same way when Jesus came as light into the darkness. God took on flesh and dwelt among us (John 1:14). Think about it. Jesus—being holy, perfect, and righteous—came into the darkness of sin to be a light.

Jesus showed us what it means to be set apart, to be sanctified. He was holy, but He existed right in the middle of the most broken, sinful, and vulnerable people. The religious leaders of Jesus' time hated Him because they thought being sanctified and holy meant hiding away from the world so as not to become tainted by the "unclean." Their version of being sanctified looked different from how Jesus embodied it.

The religious leaders of the time saw only two options. You were either elevated above everyone else in your self-righteousness or plunged into the depths because of your worldliness. The teaching on what it meant to be sanctified by the religious leaders of the time elevated the holy people above everyone else. They believed that they were better because they followed the moral law and obeyed religious commands. If you did not live in that high, holy place, you were diminished to a lowly status. You lived a synchronized life with the rest of the world, and there was no difference between you and rebellion and sin.

Jesus, however, perfectly embodied what it meant to be sanctified. That is, He lived among all that chaos and confusion in a space of grace. In that place, the Father was doing His work in Jesus and displaying Himself through Jesus. It is just as Jesus prayed for His disciples:

> *My prayer is **not** that you take them **out** of the world but that you **protect** them from the evil one. They are not of the world, even as I am not of it. Sanctify them by the truth; your word is truth. As you sent me into the world, I have sent them **into the world**. For them I sanctify myself, that they too may be truly **sanctified**.*
> *—John 17:15–19 (emphasis added)*

It is right into the world—in the middle of sin, brokenness, and suffering—where God rushes with His grace and sanctifies you. He creates space for you, protects you, and uses your journey through this world to shape you into His likeness.

A Space of Grace

Remember Kendrick, whose first love is to create music? Instead of playing, he's grinding away at his construction job. He feels like he was made for more than just his day job.

When Jesus shines into Kendrick's world as the true light, He begins a work of sanctification in him. But Kendrick does not get pulled out of his job to do music full-time. Rather, God begins to give him a new view of his work, workplace, and music. Jesus does not take him out of his circumstances; He sanctifies him in the middle of them. God makes a space of grace in the tension.

He doesn't change the circumstances. He gives Kendrick a new perspective and purpose within his circumstances.

Consider Rosa, who had dreams of being a psychologist until she met Jose. Her marriage had become a prison. But when Jesus sets her free, she does not divorce Jose or immediately become a psychologist. She begins to see her life through a different lens. She begins to see a space of grace within the place she once considered a prison.

Rosa's husband and children begin to experience a woman set free and being sanctified. She starts using her gifts at home and waits on God to see if He will open different doors for her in the future. She no longer resents the space she is in, and she is able to flourish right in the midst of circumstances she once felt bound by. Now she is able to see her husband, children, and home through eyes of freedom.

Perhaps we're like Kendrick and Rosa, prone to doing only things that get noticed, are celebrated, or are our passions—stuff we think will make us happy. We want the high-profile, popular, and fun jobs. Like Kendrick, we may want to make music, but only if we have a big enough audience and if the production comes together quickly. Like Rosa, we may want the career without the responsibility of the gifts God chooses to give us.

But God wants to make you come alive right where you are. He wants to change the way you see the life you live, the people around you, and the work you do. He wants you to be empowered to live, love, and grow in all circumstances, even the ones that seem less than ideal to you. He wants to be your space of grace in the midst of chaos.

The Sanctifying Power
of Humble Service

My view of ministry used to be flawed. I wanted to preach but only felt it was worth it if the crowd was large enough and the people gave me validation. I was in it for the recognition, for the pride of doing something big and significant. No matter how large my church was or how big the budget was, I was constantly weighed down by the sense that I needed more. I justified my selfish desires by calling them "God's will."

When God set me free from my "bondage of more," I realized that He had given me more than I could ask, dream, or imagine (Ephesians 3:20). He did not give me the more I thought I wanted, but He changed my heart and showed me the space of grace in which I lived. I was filled with contentment and began to see that the gospel was more than enough. No matter how little or much I had, no matter how low or high the attendance, I could do all things through Christ, who gave me the strength (Philippians 4:11–13).

If we're honest, the struggle I faced is shared by humanity. Humanity is selfish at its core. It's rare to find people who are willing to do humble acts of service, but this is what Christ frees us to do! Our desire for greatness keeps us from appreciating the sanctifying power of humble service. Jesus shows us a better way:

> *Jesus called them together and said, "You know that the rulers of the Gentiles lord it over them, and their high officials exercise authority over them. Not so with you. Instead, whoever wants to become great among you must be your servant, and whoever wants to be first must*

be your slave—just as the Son of Man did not come to be served, but to serve, and to give his life as a ransom for many."

*—**Matthew** 20:25–28*

If we want to be great in God's kingdom, we need to see the freedom and power of serving rather than chasing our own glory. Some of us are fooled into thinking that we have great intentions, but if we are honest, we are chasing greatness rather than our God-given purposes. I was freed when God showed me what true greatness is in the kingdom—being a servant like Jesus!

Jesus makes us more like Himself when He sanctifies us. He was the perfect model of serving all the way to the point of His death, for the glory of His Father and out of love for the world.

Have this mind among yourselves, which is yours in Christ Jesus, who, though he was in the form of God, did not count equality with God a thing to be grasped, but emptied himself, by taking the form of a servant, being born in the likeness of men. And being found in human form, he humbled himself by becoming obedient to the point of death, even death on a cross. Therefore God has highly exalted him and bestowed on him the name that is above every name, so that at the name of Jesus every knee should bow, in heaven and on earth and under the earth, and every tongue confess that Jesus Christ is Lord, to the glory of God the Father.

*—**Philippians** 2:5–11 (ESV)*

We often are not reaching what God has called us to do because we are not submitting and serving in the places of preparation where He has us. We are waiting for the day when things are public, celebrated, and fun. But God is doing a deeply important work in us in the waiting and in the hidden, secret places. We need to trust Him even when we cannot see what He is doing.

We serve a God who uses the foolish to confound the wise and the weak to confound the strong (1 Corinthians 1:27). He is a God who exalts the humble (James 4:10). If He starts something, He will finish it (Philippians 1:6).

The Purpose of the Space

The heavens are telling of the glory of God; and their expanse is declaring the work of His hands.

—Psalm 19:1 *(NASB)*

Jesus did the work, and now, by His Spirit, He creates a new humanity within the confusion of this world. His people are placed in a space of grace and empowered by the Spirit to live as God's people. We are the church, not because we are separated from the world but because we live in the chosen space, protected by the grace of God and filled with the Spirit of God. We are the ones called to walk according to His Word, by His grace, in this world.

We, the church, are feeling this tension all around us every day. Should we live piously, above the chaos, or sink deep into it? Hear me when I say that those are not the only two options you have! There is a third option. God made a place of grace for you to live protected within the chaos, being sanctified. He doesn't lift you out and float you above the world; He shapes you within it!

You must exist in a space of grace where God can make you like Himself, but what it looks like to live this out is hard to explain. Like the second day of creation, this season of preparation is often not celebrated because it is not understood.

So instead of trying to explain it, I am going to explain why God does it this way. What is the purpose of the space? Why doesn't God just destroy it all and put everyone into a new world? Why does He make space in the chaos and not just eliminate it? Why does God choose a people, set them apart, and leave them in the world? I am sure that there are many reasons, but there are two powerful ones on which I have meditated.

1. He does it to sustain His creation. In terms of the actual space God made for His creation, the waters became the atmosphere creation needed to thrive. I am in awe and wonder at how God used the chaos of the waters to create a greenhouse effect to grow and sustain His creation. It produced the perfect environment for life to grow.

We can also apply this concept to our spiritual lives because we need the perfect amount of tension to grow in our new lives. God creates a perfect environment for us to grow, and He uses the chaos of this world to continue to care for, sustain, and keep His creation. "And we know that in all things God works for the good of those who love him, who have been called according to his purpose" (Romans 8:28).

2. He does it to show off His work. You will not know your created purpose apart from knowing your Creator. You will find freedom when you see that you are meant to live for God's glory rather than your own glory. God wants you not only to see and know His glory, but also to reveal His glory in the world!

In Psalm 19, David sang a song of praise and used the same word for "expanse" that is used in Genesis 1:6 (ESV) to show the purpose of this expanse. God made the expanse to show off His work. The work He created for His glory needs a space in which to be displayed. He wants to show you off to the world. You are His artwork that He wants to put on display.

Step Two of God's Creative Process: God Makes a Space

God makes a space because He wants to show you off. We are the people who see His glory in the light of Jesus, and we get to display His glory in the midst of chaos. God wants you to know His glory and show His glory. God wants to put you right in the midst of the world for all to see. Your life declares that God creates and that He is worthy to be praised. You become a light to the nations. Our new-creation humanity shows the rest of humanity what true humanity looks like.

This is the second step in God's creative process as He makes you a new creation. This is what He did in me! I did not leave my marriage, abandon my kids, quit my job, or leave the ministry. God used the tension of life to become a place of preparation and sanctification so that I could show off His work. In this space, I could display what He wanted to do in me for His glory and not what I was trying to create out of myself with selfish motivation.

I am confident that God wants to set you free from the things that bind you and hold you back. There may be things you need to walk away from and stop doing, but you are not being called to leave this world and hide away in a cave. You also aren't being called to climb a ladder to God by following a list of laws and commands.

You are being called to follow Jesus! God calls you into a space of grace where He will hold you. In that space, He will do the work of re-creating you right in the midst of the chaos in your life.

We may not understand how this part of God's creative process operates, and we may not get why it matters for our spiritual formation. But I pray that it changes the way you see what it means to be sanctified and changes how you walk through this life. You are not always going to see a major change of circumstances in your life, but you are going to see God give you grace in your circumstances. He is going to use the struggle to bring the revelation that His grace is sufficient.

Jesus said to His disciples, "Follow me, and I will *make* you..." (Matthew 4:19 ESV, emphasis added). Being in a relationship with Jesus is not about being removed from the world; it is about following Him and letting Him shape you in the middle of the tension of this world. Sanctification—God sanctifying you—is not about getting outside of the world; it is about Him making a space for you. It is about Him preparing a table for you in the presence of your enemies (Psalm 23:5). Jesus *makes* you as you follow Him.

When you begin this journey of following Jesus, remember that He called you and He will make you. He started this work, and He will continue it until its completion (Philippians 1:6). Follow Jesus, and He will provide the grace you need and make a space in the midst of everything to do His work in you.

Chapter Two Prompts

If not for the grace and power of God,
you would be crushed by the waters of chaos.

Meditate on these Scripture verses: Genesis 1:6–8; Genesis 7:11–12; Psalm 19:1.

Ponder:

* Every day of creation is initiated by the voice of God.

* The church is God's new-creation people on display in the midst of chaos.

* The second day of creation is not one that can be fully explained with words, but in it God's holiness and protection are displayed. Ask Him to teach you the depth and beauty of what He is doing in this created space.

_____

_____

_____

_____

_____

_____

_____

_____

_____

_____

_____

_____

_____

Questions: An artist sets up a workspace for creating art, an athlete has to practice in order to play well, and for a tradesman, most of the job is prep work. What is the prep work that God is doing in your life? As important as preparation is, what makes it difficult for you?

_____

_____

_____

_____

_____

_____

_____

_____

_____

_____

_____

_____

Prayer: Think about how God is protecting and preparing you. Write a prayer thanking God for the things He is doing in your life that go unnoticed.

_____

_____

_____

_____

_____

_____

_____

_____

_____

_____

Activity: Visio Divina—"divine seeing"—is an activity that invites you to encounter God through images. Look for examples from artwork or photography that speak to you about the nature of God's peace. Jot down the thoughts they evoke.

Guidelines for Visio Divina:
Approaching images with openness to God's presence.

1. Choose an image, a piece of art, or a picture.
2. Ask the Holy Spirit for illumination.
3. Quiet yourself and give all your attention to it.
4. Slowly take in every possible detail. Observe shapes, colors, shadows, lines, and empty spaces.
5. Attend to arising feelings, thoughts, and memories.
6. How do these feelings connect with your life?
7. What desires are stirring in you?
8. Journal or pray a response.
9. Close by simply resting in God's presence.

Chapter Two | *Thoughts and Drawings*

Let There Be a Foundation

*And God said, "Let the water under the sky be gathered to one place, and let **dry ground** appear." And it was so.*
—Genesis 1:9 *(emphasis added)*

*But he who received seed on the **good ground** is he who hears the word and understands it, who indeed bears fruit and produces: some a hundredfold, some sixty, some thirty."*
—Matthew 13:23 *(NKJV, emphasis added)*

Each day of creation started with "And God said," which shows that the words God spoke are just as important as who was speaking and who was creating. Because God is speaking, we can rest in and trust Him, knowing that whatever He says will happen. All that He says is good, glorious, powerful, gracious, and loving because that is who He is. God cannot lie, and when He speaks, it's true and powerful (Numbers 23:19).

On the third day of creation, God laid a foundation. I call this day "the day of the earth's foundation and vegetation." The foundation is what everything else is built upon. If the foundation is faulty, the whole structure will be faulty. If the foundation isn't strong, then nothing built upon it will last.

God separated the waters to create dry, fertile land and placed seed-bearing plants in the soil that would cause the earth to flourish. This was when God spoke to bring about the details, the elements of living, to the earth. These living elements would create oxygen in the new atmosphere and would soon be guided and nurtured by the sun. Therefore, as it says in Genesis 1:13, the evening and the morning were the third day of creation. It was good because there was more than just water on the earth; there was a foundation for everything to grow upon.

Build Upon the Rock

*Therefore everyone who hears these words of mine and puts them into practice is like a wise man who built his house on the rock. The rain came down, the streams rose, and the winds blew and beat against that house; yet it did not fall, because it had its **foundation** on the rock.*

—**Matthew 7:24–25** (emphasis added)

It seems that there are people who would rather build quickly or in beautiful, sandy locations than take the time to make sure that a solid foundation is in place. God is a master craftsman, and in order to create something beautiful, strong, and sustainable, He took a full day in His creative process to lay a foundation.

As human beings, we want the quick, easy, and aesthetically pleasing more than we want the patient, hard, and functional. We often attempt a faster and less complicated way to get our desired outcome.

I want to be an amazing musician, but I can't skip the hours of learning the foundations of music and building muscle memory. I want to be the best athlete, but it won't happen if I don't devote my life to practicing the game. I want to lose weight and be healthy, but it won't be sustainable unless I change my eating habits and develop an exercise routine. I want a great marriage filled with romance and spice, but it won't come without building a foundation of communication and trust.

Are you beginning to see the heart of the Creator and His thoughtfulness in the pattern of His creative process? We should learn to see the beauty in God's process as He makes us new creations. When we first see Jesus, we may think that everything is going to be perfect the next day, but that is not the reality of how God works. He is artistically, patiently, and thoughtfully doing His work in you, and it takes *time*. I hope that as you go through this book, you can enjoy how God is working in you today. He has finished the work in Christ, but He is not finished with you yet. He knows that nothing built in your life will last unless you have a strong foundation.

The strength of a structure lies in its foundation. A foundation has at least three basic purposes: (1) to support the load of the entire structure; (2) to keep occupants and buildings safe during havoc and from forces of nature; and (3) to protect from waters below, which could weaken the structure over time. A poorly constructed foundation can be dangerous to the occupants and the entire neighborhood.

Jesus used this same illustration in Matthew 7. The one who builds his or her house upon a rock has a strong foundation in the storms of life. You build your house upon the rock by hearing the Word of God and putting it into practice (Matthew 7:24).

God will not create something without first preparing a foundation, which is why each step of creation is so perfectly planned. God didn't create man while the world was still submerged in darkness and chaos, and He didn't place Adam on land devoid of life.

Even David understood what God was doing on the third day. He sang, "For he laid the earth's foundation on the seas and built it on the ocean depths" (Psalm 24:2 NLT). If God was going to create something strong, He could not build upon water; it had to be on something stable, a firm foundation.

A Foundation of Faith

Then God said, "Let the land produce vegetation: seed-bearing plants and trees on the land that bear fruit with seed in it, according to their various kinds." And it was so. The land produced vegetation: plants bearing seed according to their kinds and trees bearing fruit with seed in it according to their kinds. And God saw that it was good. And there was evening, and there was morning—the third day.
—***Genesis 1:11–13***

When God created the world, it needed a foundation. Similarly, when God makes you a new creation, you need a foundation. God prepared the ground, the foundation, for the purpose of producing fruit. This is what we see happening in the second part of the third day of creation. God prepared the ground and then caused it to spring up with vegetation.

The foundation of our relationship with God is faith. In Matthew 7:24, Jesus said, "Therefore everyone who hears these words of mine and puts them into practice is like a wise man who built his house on the rock." In other words, putting God's Word into action is the product of faith. Faith is the soil in which God's Word is planted and how He brings about vegetation to sustain you as a new creation.

"Without faith it is impossible to please God" (Hebrews 11:6). Without faith, you cannot know God or build any type of life with Jesus. Faith is the solid foundation you need in order to have a strong, healthy, and sustained life as a new creation in Christ.

When God does the work of making you a new creation, He is going to give you the gift of faith, on which everything in your life will be built. I think the more understandable word in our language for faith is *trust*. Jesus is the cornerstone and the strength of that foundation. There is no way I can accurately describe how essential faith is and how foundational it is to all God wants to do in your life, but I can try to illustrate by sharing my story.

"Just Have Faith"

When I was a kid, if I thought something was amazing, I would say, "That is *bad*." I would say that word so often! I remember my dad looking at me and making "old people" comments about how he didn't get my slang. He would use a mocking teenage voice and say, "That's bad!" I would laugh at him like he didn't get it.

That experience came to my mind when my teenage sons started using slang. They would say something was "sick" to mean that it was cool. I took cues from my pops and mocked them about how it didn't make sense.

I know that's a silly example for a real problem, but it is interesting to me that we redefine words by using a word with the opposite meaning. Why do we use *bad* or *sick* to describe something good? We live in a culture that loves to redefine words, but in doing that, we lose the meaning for some very rich words.

This is what worries me about the word *faith*. I think that we have changed the definition. Let me explain what I mean. I was once going through a hard time in life when everything was changing and all that I had worked for was being ripped from underneath me. The church tribe I was involved with at the time used the word *faith* all the time. Every time I was at church, people would tell me, "Just have faith."

I was in so much pain, and every time they said it, I would become infuriated. I told my wife, "If someone tells me one more time to have faith, I am going to go off." During that difficult season of my life, faith seemed so cold and distant. It just sounded like oversimplified, insensitive, positive thinking and words. I was tired of pretending that everything was good when I was struggling.

I got so fed up that the next time someone said it to me, I quoted a line from *The Princess Bride*. I said in my best Inigo Montoya voice, "You keep using that word. I do not think it means what you think it means."[2]

Faith was being taught to me as something I had to confess and proclaim. I realized that to those around me, faith meant speaking the right things or practicing positive confessions. In American Christianity, faith means having a correct set of beliefs.

If faith is our foundation, the enemy has done an amazing job at redefining it, so we don't even know what it means.

This experience of feeling the effects of the word *faith* being so misused in my life sent me into a season of seeking God to help me understand faith. I hope this chapter can be used to help you see what faith is and to give you a deeper understanding of why you cannot move into the next steps in your growth process unless you have a firm foundation of faith.

Faith Comes by Hearing

Let me take you on a journey that changed my life, a journey that will help you to understand faith and the foundation that God wants to create and lay in you. James 2:14–26 indicates that faith is made complete through our actions, our obedience. Jude 1:20 exhorts us to build our lives on a foundation of faith, directed by the Holy Spirit. Matthew 28:19–20 tells us to keep investing, to make disciples and teach them to obey all that has been commanded.

When I was feeling lost and confused about faith, God had my heart resonate with the prayer of His disciples in Luke 17:5: "Increase our faith!" Over and over, Jesus told His disciples not to sin against others or cause them to stumble and to forgive those who sinned against them.

They realized that they did not have it in them to do what He asked, so they cried out for more faith. You might be praying about this as you hear what God has called you to do. Maybe it seems like too large a goal. Perhaps what you're facing seems too hard, and you feel like it's impossible to believe God. You, too, can pray, "Increase my faith!"

In the same passage, Jesus launched into a famous parable that I think is best translated in The Message:

> But the Master said, "You don't need more faith. There is no 'more' or 'less' in faith. If you have a bare kernel of faith, say the size of a poppy seed, you could say to this sycamore tree, 'Go jump in the lake,' and it would do it."
>
> —*Luke 17:6*(MSG)

It's important to talk about a seed when we're looking at the third day of creation because that's when God planted seeds into soil.

Another biblical passage which illustrates this concept is found in Matthew 13:

> Therefore hear the parable of the sower: When anyone hears the word of the kingdom, and does not understand it, then the wicked one comes and snatches away what was sown in his heart. This is he who received seed by the wayside. But he who received the seed on stony places, this is he who hears the word and immediately receives it with joy; yet he has no root in himself, but endures only for a while. For when tribulation or persecution arises because of the word, immediately he stumbles. Now he who received seed among the thorns is he who hears the word, and the cares of this world and the deceitfulness of riches choke the word, and he becomes unfruitful. But he who received seed on the good ground is he who hears the word and understands it, who indeed bears fruit and produces: some a hundredfold, some sixty, some thirty."
>
> —*Matthew 13:18–23* (NKJV)

In this passage, Jesus described what kind of foundation believers ought to have for God to be able to do His work in them. In order for God to produce fruit in your life, you need *good ground*. According to this passage, good ground is when you hear His Word and understand it.

The earth's seed is in itself. The power of that seed to grow and multiply lies in the strength of the foundation the seed has. Jesus taught His disciples about faith because, like most of the world today, they knew they needed to have faith, but they might not have known what it was. They might not have known how powerful a seed like faith could be.

Luke 17:6 says that we should "have faith *as* a mustard seed" (NKJV, emphasis added), not *the size of* a mustard seed. If Jesus had taught His disciples that they could have a small amount of faith, He would have been contradicting Himself when He rebuked them for having so little faith (Matthew 8:26). This passage is not about the size of faith (as illustrated in The Message translation); it is about knowing what faith really is.

Jesus shared the story of a servant in Luke 17:7–10 to explain faith. In order for us to understand faith, we have to understand the master-servant relationship. In the parable, the servant only did what he was commanded to do and did not expect thanks for it. The disciples asked for more faith, and Jesus taught them that they did not need more. Rather, they needed to understand that faith was the ability to hear and do what the master was telling them to do. When we obey our Master, we are only fulfilling our duty, so we should not be seeking praise for ourselves. The power is in His Word, and we obey it for His glory.

In short, I think faith is:

1.   Trusting in your authority.

2.   Listening.

3.   Obeying.

4.   Having the right heart.

The foundation of your covenant relationship with God is hearing His voice and doing whatever He tells you, trusting in His Word. Our Master, Jesus, is not like the masters of this world—He serves us way more than we have ever or will ever serve Him!

Understanding this truth turned my world upside down. I realized that faith is not about me saying the right positive sentiments or trying harder not to doubt. It is not about me thinking deeper or becoming smarter. Faith is about hearing.

Romans 10:17 says, "So then faith comes by hearing, and hearing by the word of God" (NKJV). Therefore, we shouldn't strive to muster up enough faith; we should simply open our ears and hear His Word. We need faith to live out what we hear from God's Word. Great things can happen because our faith is in God. God's Word has power, and whatever God says can happen. Remember, the whole world was created by His Word!

So often we try to increase our faith rather than simply resting and being faithful in what God has called us to do. Those who hear His Word and understand it are the ones with good ground, a good foundation, where fruit will grow.

A New Foundation

Remember lovesick Carl? When God revealed Himself to Carl, he found himself satisfied in Christ. He saw for the first time that he was making a god out of marriage. He realized that he was not trusting Jesus, but he was trying to use Him to get married.

His revelation of Jesus did not take away his desire for marriage but gave him a greater affection for Jesus. He trusted that if it was God's will, he would be married. He found rest in the waiting that came from this new foundation of faith.

Rosa was a frustrated wife and mother, but when she allowed God to lay a foundation of faith in her, she was able to hear God's Word and live it out in her life. She realized that she could use her gifts of discernment and communication to build and grow her relationships with her family. Rosa had been looking outside of what God gave her when she needed to look inside of what God gave her. Even in Rosa's disappointment about the timing, she could depend on Christ as her strong foundation. If He promised work in the field she desired, then He would open up doors. She would rest in waiting to hear His voice for the next steps she should take.

Remember the Order

It is hard for me to teach this step of God's creative process without reminding you of the order. You cannot start here, at this step, or you will become legalistic, thinking that you must listen and obey to earn God's love and grace. This is far from true, and it's out of God's order! Faith does not come before God's love and grace. God showed His love *first*, before you ever responded to Him, before a foundation of faith was laid. He already made a space of grace for you to live in.

Change comes from heart transformation, and God is the One who, in His love, transforms a dark and empty heart. We are not saved because of our works but because of God's grace.

Faith is a gift that flows from seeing God's love and grace. Our trust is manifested by listening to and obeying His Word. However, listening and obeying is not our identity as children of God. Our identity is that we are loved by God the Father and made His own by grace. Our response to that is trust, and our trust is manifested when we listen to and obey God's leading.

Step Three of God's Creative Process: Laying a Foundation

The third step of God's creative process is laying a foundation from which His Word can grow and produce fruit in you. Living by faith means trusting God by hearing His Word and putting it into practice, because "faith without deeds is dead" (James 2:26). The delight of obeying the Father's Word is the foundation, the solid ground, of this new created life.

As beloved children, we have to learn to listen and do. When we see God creating in us with His words, it should deepen our love for His Word, His voice that flows from His character. It is because of who He is that we can trust everything He says. We don't live on bread alone but on every word that comes from His mouth (Matthew 4:4).

If listening is so important, how do we hear God? Here is my simple encouragement to you: be still and listen. God is a perfect communicator, and He will make sure that you hear. So often we try to figure out the right way to hear, but if you have a desire to hear, rest assured that you have a good Father who will make sure that His children know His voice (John 10:4). Trust Him to make His Word clear.

If you believe that He has said something to you, then make sure that it is submitted to His written Word to validate it and to His community to confirm and discern it. Be patient as you walk out each step. Trust Him because if He said it—no matter what you see with your eyes—He will do it.

I do not want this to sound like oversimplified rules, but I encourage you to "be quick to listen" (James 1:19). Spend time in the Bible, listening to God's voice. Spend time listening in prayer. Spend time in community, listening to His people. Your loving Father, who has been speaking since the beginning, will make His voice clear to you.

Learn from the faith Peter had when he stepped out onto the water: "Say the word, and I will come to you" (Matthew 14:28, paraphrase). We should have this prayer as the foundation of our walk with God: "Father, I will not move until You say the word! Speak, Lord, and I will listen." Your faith rests in God's ability to speak and accomplish what He says. Even though Peter did not walk perfectly, he listened when Jesus spoke. When Peter was sinking, Jesus lifted him, corrected him, and used him. The power is not in your perfect walk; it is in God's Word and grace.

Chapter Three Prompts

You can trust who God is and what He says
because of His character.

Meditate on these Scripture verses: Genesis 1:9–13; Matthew 7:24–27; Luke 17:5–10; Romans 10:17; James 2:26.

Ponder:

* Think about God being the giver of all things. Journal what that says about His character.

* Write down what you think a relationship without trust and faith would look like.

* As a loving child, you want to hear and obey your Father. That is faith: hearing and doing. Journal what this means to you and how it changes your life.

Questions: What forms the foundation of your life? In what ways can you continue to hear God's Word and obey it?

Prayer: Sit with your Father and listen. What is He telling you to do? Write down the simplest things as well as the bigger things. What does obeying Him look like for your life today?

_____

_____

_____

_____

_____

_____

_____

_____

_____

_____

_____

_____

Activity: Take a nature walk and find a seed from any plant or tree. Hold the seed up next to the plant or tree from which it came. Think about the fact that something big came from a small seed. Remember that when God looks at the seed, He sees the fully grown tree or plant. Tape the seed in your journal, then snap a picture of what it will look like fully grown. Tape that photo next to the seed.

Chapter Three | *Thoughts and Drawings*

Let There Be Seasons

*And God said, "Let there be lights in the expanse of the heavens to separate the day from the night. And let them be for signs and for **seasons**, and for days and years, and let them be lights in the expanse of the heavens to give light upon the earth." And it was so.*
—*Genesis 1:14–15* (ESV, emphasis added)

*There is a **time** for everything, and a **season** for every activity under the heavens....*
—*Ecclesiastes 3:1* (emphasis added)

I was 20 when I met my future wife at the Bible institute we both attended. She was the best thing I got from going to Bible college. As our relationship deepened and we began talking of getting married, our friends, family, and community advised us not to do it for a lot of good reasons. Trying to be open to their concerns, we listened and sought to receive their words, but we both knew that marriage was something God was leading us to do.

One day, Dr. Larry Hill, a teacher I highly respected (and still do today), said to me, "Aaron, I heard you're getting married." I braced myself for warnings, but he said, "It's going to work!"

My ears perked up, and I asked, "Why do you say that?"

He replied, "Because you understand covenant."

I am not sure if he meant it this way, but that passing line became a prophetic word that sent me on a journey to study and understand covenant. I learned so much about covenant that went beyond marriage.

I discovered that covenant originated in the character of God and that He is deeply committed to and in love with those with whom He is in covenant. One of the key things I learned was that a covenant relationship embeds into its vows a promise to be committed to each other no matter what happens.

I remember looking at my bride on August 22, 1998, as we said our covenant vows to each other. I was not hoping for bad times or planning for them, but I knew that bad and good things were going to happen. Things in our marriage would change, and we would go through high and low seasons in our marriage journey. But one thing I could not change was my commitment, my covenant relationship, with my bride.

My relationship with her would illuminate my life because we would be an influence, a luminary, for each other. A luminary is a reflection of the true light of God, and I knew we would be that for each other in all seasons of life.

In the covenant language of relationships, there's an embedded reality that no matter what happens, for better or worse, we're committed to each other. We're going to love one another for the rest of our lives. That concept fights everything our culture craves. We want everything in our lives to be a progressive climb that gets better and better. When we plan out our businesses and our lives, we plan for exponential increase, growth, and prosperity. We almost always believe that it will happen as we move forward.

Because of cultural cravings, there is grave danger in preaching a false gospel that says God's role is to make us healthy, wealthy, and wise. Some teach that God desires for us to have only good days and that life will only get better and better so long as we say and do the right things.

This kind of preaching turns God into a means to an end rather than the end in Himself. We misunderstand who we are in our relationship with Jesus if we believe that putting our faith in Christ is a single step that results in our every wish coming true.

We need God to be our Father, not our genie in a magic bottle. We need Him to hear our cry and respond as He sees fit. It is better for us to have God, His kingdom, and His will than it is for us to have ourselves, our comfort, and our way. We get to rejoice in our new covenant relationship with God because of Jesus. No matter what season we are experiencing in life, *we have Him.*

With that covenant promise in our hearts, we should look at our relationship with Christ as an ongoing act of creation. Just as God's fourth act of creation was to order things by times and seasons, His fourth act of creating in our lives calls us into a discerning of times and seasons. We are able to grow and learn as we experience all He has for us in our lives.

In becoming these new creations in our journey with Christ, as we go into a covenant relationship with God, it would be a step of great wisdom to learn the value of times and seasons because they are built into our covenant with Him. Our relationship with God is a "nothing can separate us" type of love (Romans 8:38–39). That means we will walk with Him through changing seasons, but He will give us lights, or luminaries, in every season to sustain and lead us.

God Is Our Luminary in Every Season

And God said, "Let there be lights in the vault of the sky to separate the day from the night, and let them serve as signs to mark sacred times, and days and years, and let them be lights in the vault of the sky to give light on the earth." And it was so. God made two great lights—the greater light to govern the day and the lesser light to govern the night. He also made the stars. God set them in the vault of the sky to give light on the earth, to govern the day and the night, and to separate light from darkness. And God saw that it was good. And there was evening, and there was morning—the fourth day.

—Genesis 1:14–19

On the first day of creation, God said, "Let there be light" (Genesis 1:3). But it was not until the fourth day that He said, "Let there be the sun, moon, and stars." There was a source of light before there were luminaries to reflect that source.

When I came to the fourth day of creation in my study, I was caught in a place of wonder that the uncreated earth had light without the sun, moon, or stars. I think this is powerful because many people have worshipped the sun for years as the source of light and life. But God's Word brought light, and He is the source of true light (John 8:12).

God is like the greater light, the sun, that illuminates the earth. I want you to look at Jesus as the center that holds all things in place. Jesus said, "Anyone who has seen me has seen the Father" (John 14:9). We have to see the light of God in the face of Jesus if we are going to understand times and seasons.

This picture helped me to look at the body of Christ as the lesser light, the moon, with diverse gifts reflecting the greater light. I will give more examples of this later in the chapter. As beautiful as it is that God gives us lesser lights, let me take a minute to warn you of a danger.

Problems happen when we look at luminaries and think that they are the light rather than a reflection of the true light. Light reflected off a mirror is not the light; it is just a reflection. When you start to look at it as the source, you will miss the point of luminaries. You will start to worship created things instead of the Creator (Romans 1:25).

Deuteronomy 4:19 shows us that we need to be careful not to elevate man or creation above God: "And beware lest you raise your eyes to heaven, and when you see the sun and the moon and the stars, all the host of heaven, you be drawn away and bow down to them and serve them, things that the LORD your God has allotted to all the peoples under the whole heaven" (ESV).

Let the luminaries of Scripture give light. God sends luminaries to guide you through the dark seasons of life, but when you depend on leaders, prophets, and teachers instead of on Him, you can easily be led astray. You will be let down and become discouraged. Many times I have seen people look at others in their lives who are reflecting the light of Jesus and begin to think that they are the light.

Ultimately, the moon has no light of its own; it reflects the light of the sun. So it is with our relationship with Christ and how God created the world in systematic order.

Seasons and Growth

On the third day of creation, God prepared good ground and planted seeds. In His divine design, He established that growth could only come from the cycle of changing seasons. In the natural world, our seasons cycle through winter, spring, summer, and fall. Every season serves a specific purpose in the creation of life and its growth.

I will be honest: in the natural, I hate fall and winter. This is why I currently live in Phoenix and probably will stay there for life. People in cooler climates would laugh at what I, as a desert-dweller, call cold, but when it is cold, I get grumpy. The cold weather of winter and fall feels absent of light and warmth. When I travel to colder places and see true fall, I notice how everything seems to begin to die. Winter can bring harsh winds and icy ground. When I experience it, I want to run home to Phoenix because I cannot see how life can thrive in those conditions.

However, all of these seasons have a role to play in the overall cycle of life. It is in the cold, seemingly lifeless time when the ground and trees are prepared to host new life, new fruit. There would be no growth without these harsh seasons.

See! The winter is past; the rains are over and gone. Flowers appear on the earth; the season of singing has come, the cooing of doves is heard in our land. The fig tree forms its early fruit; the blossoming vines spread their fragrance.

—Song of Songs 2:11–13a

When light and warmth begin to resurface again in the spring, that is when the signs of new life emerge. God created the seasons to cause seeds to grow. In the same way, we go through many seasons in our life cycle, and each one is strategically designed to produce fruit in our lives.

Without different seasons, you would not grow. Without the testing of your faith, you would not mature. Seasons are God's gift of growth. In the dark, cold times, it is easy to lose sight of the luminaries God gives you to see, to know, to learn, and to remind you that He is there with you. Even in the darkest of times, remember that God will provide a luminary to light the way for you.

God Doesn't Stop Times and Seasons

There is a time for everything, and a season for every activity under the heavens: a time to be born and a time to die, a time to plant and a time to uproot, a time to kill and a time to heal, a time to tear down and a time to build, a time to weep and a time to laugh, a time to mourn and a time to dance, a time to scatter stones and a time to gather them, a time to embrace and a time to refrain from embracing, a time to search and a time to give up, a time to keep and a time to throw away, a time to tear and a time to mend, a time to be silent and a time to speak, a time to love and a time to hate, a time for war and a time for peace.

—Ecclesiastes 3:1–8

Seasons are a reality of life, but we often do not see their value or purpose. When we are in fun seasons—times of embracing, collecting, and laughing—we can recognize them as wonderful seasons. But we often miss the value and purpose of a season when things aren't going well or feeling good.

If we are honest, we'll admit that we would like God to give us only things we would choose. Our faith is most often tested when we hit dark seasons. I cannot tell you how many times I have heard others say, "I have done everything right, God. You owe me."

We want a God who will always keep us in the easy seasons, but that isn't the way life works. There are easy seasons and challenging seasons. If we recognize that the dark seasons are there to grow us, create in us, and perfect us, then they aren't really bad seasons at all.

False gospels promise, "If you give your life to Jesus, you will always have warm, sunny days and happiness." When the dark seasons come, they cry out, "God is a liar!"

When I look through the Bible for someone who actually understood the times and seasons, Solomon seems to be the best example. Solomon had everything. He makes the richest person of today look foolish. Solomon looked at everything he owned and called it all vanity (Ecclesiastes 2:11 ESV). It was meaningless. It was vapor. Solomon knew that it would all pass away. He understood times and seasons.

Many people strive to be in places of wealth and power, like Solomon, but it takes real wisdom and discernment to see that material possessions and worldly status were never designed to fulfill us. The things of this earth are not eternal; they are seasonal. It takes maturity and revelation for us to see that all we have is from God. We are called to steward everything God gives us in season and out of season.

Luminaries in Season

Even after Carl finally found a wife, he did not experience the happiness in marriage that he dreamed he would. What Carl didn't realize was that God was doing something in his life through the difficulty he experienced in his season of singleness. In the silence and the loneliness, God was at work.

Now, in marriage, Carl needs to see that unless God is the true fulfillment in his life, he will never know contentment in singleness or in marriage. Both seasons serve a purpose and need to be stewarded. Carl's wife reminds him that she is only a luminary pointing him back to God, the source of true light and satisfaction.

When we think of times and seasons, we don't often connect them with luminaries, but we should. As I meditated on the creation story and saw that God gave luminaries in times and seasons, I also saw a pattern of God giving us luminaries in different seasons of our lives. God sends His people, as lesser lights, to lead and guide us in the midst of different seasons. He has provided prophets, priests, leaders, and apostles as lights pointing us to Him. These luminaries are not the source of light but are meant to bear witness to the Light. John 1:8 tells us that John the Baptist was sent as a reflection to bear witness of Jesus, who is the true Light: "He himself was not the light; he came only as a witness to the light."

God is going to take you through many seasons in your covenant with Him, so learn to discern seasons and times. In all of this, God will continue to show His light. Even in dark seasons, there will be flickers of hope.

Remember how Hope felt hopeless because she had been abused? When Jesus became the light of her life, she experienced a love she had never known before. She thought all of the abuse and darkness from her past would be wiped away in an instant, and she felt so much shame when she had flashbacks and haunting thoughts of her childhood. Even after she got married and had children, triggers would transport her back to those experiences. She struggled with feeling like everything God had done in her life was for nothing.

Yet in the dark seasons of her life, God places lesser lights to remind her of His great light. She has a husband who loves her deeply and is not going anywhere. She has children through whom she can see the life of Christ flowing. She has a church that has cried with her and pointed her back to her new life in Jesus. In every season of healing and growth, she has had luminaries reminding her that God is "an ever-present help in trouble" (Psalm 46:1).

Times and seasons will change because growth is not a means to an end; growth is becoming, more and more, who you already are in Christ. Christ is the end, not the means to an end. He is everything.

Discerning Seasons and Times

I pray that as you're going through this book, you are able to discern the times and seasons in which God has placed you. I pray that you learn to walk in covenant with Him and that you enter into that time of saying, "No matter what comes, I'm in a covenant relationship with the God of the universe. No matter what season of life I'm in, He will sustain me because He is making me into this new creation."

God will give you luminaries to help you understand your seasons, something constant that continues to shine. I would like to be a luminary for you for a moment and share three main lessons I want you to understand about seasons.

1. Do not get stuck in a season, and do not skip a season. Each season leads to the next season, so you shouldn't get stuck in a season. Don't quit and say, "It's too hard. I'm not going to do it." If you stay in a season, you will grow stagnant and stunt your growth. If you skip a season, you will not learn what is necessary to grow in your continued covenant relationship with Christ.

The only way you will avoid getting stuck in a season or skipping a season is if you learn that God's Word is what moves you in and out of seasons. Learn to wait, listen, and be patient.

2. Every season has a purpose. Have you ever gone through a hard season and wondered about its purpose? You probably didn't discover the purpose until you looked back at the situation after you had walked through it. Hindsight is 20/20, allowing you to have perfect vision in retrospect. Sometimes when looking back, you can see that a difficult season brought about incredible spiritual development and that God was indeed working despite the darkness.

This was true for me, and I believe that it's true for all mature Christians. It is in the hard times that we see the most growth. We may not understand our dark times in the moment, but later we can see how God used them for His glory and our good. I think this is why the apostle Paul took joy in trials. He knew that God was doing something in the midst of those difficult seasons.

3. Each season leads to the next season. If you are not born, you cannot die. If you do not plant, you cannot pluck. If there isn't a time to tear down, you won't see a time of building. Without the previous season, the new season would not make sense. No season lasts indefinitely, for each season leads you into the upcoming season. Each season prepares you so that you are ready for the growth to come in the next season.

The season you are in right now, no matter how bad or good it feels, will not last. But in order for you to reach a new level, you have to understand the purpose of the season. When God said, "The latter ... shall be greater than the former" (Haggai 2:9 ESV), He did not mean that you would never go through hard times. He meant that He would always build upon past seasons to bring you into the new season.

Step Four of God's Creative Process:
Grow Through Changing Seasons

*Do all things without grumbling or disputing, that you may be blameless and innocent, children of God without blemish in the midst of a crooked and twisted generation, among whom you **shine as lights in the world**, holding fast to the word of life, so that in the day of Christ I may be proud that I did not run in vain or labor in vain.*

—*Philippians 2:14–16* *(ESV, emphasis added)*

The fourth step of God's creative process is to grow you through the varying seasons of life so you can be a luminary to a world still in darkness. Think of the people in your life who have pointed you to God. God puts people in your life to influence you in different seasons.

God sends luminaries of His light to move people through times and seasons. Prophets, judges, teachers, and apostles have served as luminaries declaring God's Word. Throughout Scripture, luminaries like Moses, Joshua, Nehemiah, Paul, and Deborah influenced others.

God will reflect His light in every season. We see this in Noah, Joseph, Moses, Isaiah, the prophets, kings, priests, Paul, and all the apostles. God positioned them at different times throughout history to point people to Him.

Jesus said to His disciples, "I am the light of the world" (John 8:12), but He also told them, "You are the light of the world" (Matthew 5:14). Let the light of the gospel shine through you as you use your gifts to enlighten others on this creation journey with God. Your job is to reflect the light of Jesus.

The point of being a luminary in the world is not to be seen but to let the world see a reflection of the Creator through you. As you grow deeper in your covenant with God through the various seasons of life, you will become more like the moon, shining a bright light into the dark world.

Chapter Four Prompts

Every season in life has a purpose.

Meditate on these Scripture verses: Genesis 1:14–19; Ecclesiastes 3; John 1:6–8; Deuteronomy 4:19.

Ponder:

*   You must avoid getting stuck in or skipping seasons.

*   Draw or write your thoughts about God's patience.

*   Be honest and think about how patient you are. Are there things that God is growing patiently in you? Write them out.

_____

_____

_____

_____

_____

_____

_____

_____

_____

_____

_____

_____

Questions: In what ways have you started seeing growth in your own patience and growth in your understanding of God's patience? Why are difficult seasons important in life? What lights has God used to remind you of Himself?

_____

_____

_____

_____

_____

_____

_____

_____

_____

_____

_____

_____

Prayer: Thank God for the luminaries in your life who are reflections of Him to you for this season. Journal a prayer asking Him to help you be a luminary to others who are facing challenging seasons.

_____

_____

_____

_____

_____

_____

_____

_____

_____

_____

_____

_____

_____

Activity: Go out at night and find a good place to look up at the moon and stars. Sit quietly and let the Lord speak to you.

Chapter Four | *Thoughts and Drawings*

Let the Earth Be Filled with Diversity

*Then God said, "Let the waters swarm with fish and other life. Let the skies be filled with birds **of every kind**."*
—***Genesis 1:20*** (NLT, emphasis added)

For just as each of us has one body with many members, and these members do not all have the same function, so in Christ we, though many, form one body, and each member belongs to all the others.
—***Romans 12:4–5***

Dana and I were so excited when we were able to buy the house of our dreams. We were going to take all the money from selling our old house and put it into making this brand-new house all we ever wanted. Dana spent days—while pregnant—on scaffolding, painting every room. We bought the furniture we wanted, we installed beautiful wood flooring, and we got a custom backyard. When we were done, it was *perfect*, and I was so excited!

Then I got nervous about moving into the house because I did not want my kids and the dog to mess everything up! I had created a perfect space, but then I did not want to fill it, especially not with something that could potentially ruin all our hard work.

Teeming with Life

By the time we reach the fifth day of creation, the world is nearly complete. Like our newly renovated house, it could almost be called perfect. But if God had stopped there, the world would have been empty, so He created some animals and people to fill it up and build a diverse community. When God created the earth with Himself at the center of the universe, He created great diversity that was brought together in Him.

My wife and I have five amazing kids, and we have always had others living with us whom we've adopted into our family. We have had dogs and all kinds of community groups in our home. Our house is always filled with life!

Built into God's created purpose for us is having a full life and being a part of a diverse and beautiful new creation in the family of God. But I think most people, like me, want everything perfectly put together in their world. We resist the idea of God filling our lives with various responsibilities or placing us in a family where we have to live as one.

Let's look again at Kendrick, who wanted to work only at music and was under the impression that would make his life full.

When God became the center of his life, he saw that he needed a fuller life. He realized that his family, his friends, his community, and even his job were valuable. He needed all of them in order to live the full life God created him to have.

He found greater context for his gift of music when he started serving his community and formed an entire record label. He didn't just make good music; he gathered all kinds of artists together for fuller community. God's plan was much broader than Kendrick's personal fulfillment.

When Rosa surrendered her life and dreams to her Creator, she found that a greater love for her husband and kids was formed in the dark seasons. She needed that growth and transformation because when God allowed her to open her own practice much later in life, it greatly impacted how she loved and served her patients. She needed to learn how to love all kinds of people. She needed a fuller view of her life. God's plans for her were not one-dimensional.

God Gives Diverse Gifts

On the fifth day of creation, God began to create life of all kinds on the earth. He created *diversity*.

Sometimes diversity leads to comparison and dissatisfaction. We see someone who has more, and we think that God owes us more, or we try to elevate ourselves above others and become the greatest. But each creature on this earth has a different role to play. Each of us has been given a uniqueness designed to glorify God.

As I meditated on this idea, I saw the same pattern in many other parts of Scripture. This parable Jesus told is one example:

Again, it will be like a man going on a journey, who called his servants and entrusted his wealth to them. To one he gave five bags of gold, to another two bags, and to another one bag, each according to his ability. Then he went on his journey. The man who had received five bags of gold went at once and put his money to work and gained five bags more. So also, the one with two bags of gold gained two more. But the man who had received one bag went off, dug a hole in the ground and hid his master's money....

Then the man who had received one bag of gold came. "Master," he said, "I knew that you are a hard man, harvesting where you have not sown and gathering where you have not scattered seed. So I was afraid and went out and hid your gold in the ground. See, here is what belongs to you."

                                            —Matthew 25:14–18, 24–25

What strikes me in this parable is that your perception of God determines how you invest His gifts. The question is not whether God will fill your life; it is how you will steward what God has filled your life with.

This parable from Matthew 25:14–30 is the greatest illustration of multiplying what's been given to you to fill God's creation and live in fullness. The master gave a varied amount of talents to his servants. He filled their lives with gifts and the ability to take something and multiply it however they wished. One servant had five talents, another two talents, and another one talent.

Perhaps you're familiar with the story. Each servant took the gold he was given and invested it, except the servant who had been given only one bag of gold. He didn't want to waste or lose what he'd been given, so he took his bag and buried it. He told the master that he had hidden the bag because he was afraid of him.

If we are afraid of the One who created us, we will bury what He has given us. We may look at others and think that God has given them more than what we have. All of us have been given roles to play in God's story, and He wants us to put them to use. But many of us are crippled by fear, pride, or comparison. This spoke to me because I am the chief of all sinners in this area.

I was in a place in my life with so many good gifts that God had given me, but I thought that God was an angry God, and I desired to be greater than everyone else. So instead of enjoying and stewarding all God gave me, I buried my anger, heaped burdens on others, and felt like I did not have enough.

For years I thought that I was meant to have the biggest church and an international ministry. I wanted people all over the world to know and respect me. I thought that God wasn't giving me what I wanted, so I got mad at Him. I was drowning in comparison and discontentment as I looked everywhere except to the face of my Maker.

I broke free only when I saw the beauty of God as my Creator in the face of Jesus. I was freed from my own self-worship and anger, and I realized the joy of having the full life God wanted for me rather than just a big, successful ministry. He stripped me all the way down to the foundation of my faith in Him and showed me all the beautiful diversity with which He filled my life.

I realized that He had given me a gift and that I fit together with all the other parts of His body, creation, and family. I was greatly humbled when I saw that God had given me more than enough to give from. I wanted to invest my whole self for His glory.

God is generous, and He gives good gifts to His children (Matthew 7:11). As you invest what He has given you, you will see that He will cause your gifts to grow and flourish, and you will present them back to Him as worship.

I have been blessed with a wife and kids. I get to pastor with my dear friends in a beautiful church family in the inner city of Phoenix. I have had a career outside of vocational ministry, which developed other useful skills in me, such as marketing, project management, and business strategy. I love to sing. I have many friends who love me, not for what I do or what I give to them but for who God has created me to be. The list could go on. It is not what I dreamed, but it is far better than I could ask, dream, or imagine (Ephesians 3:20).

My dreams made me angry at God and kept me distant from Him, but now I have received a greater revelation that His plans are better for me. He has plans for me that are better than my self-centered dreams.

I am not the most talented, most gifted, most driven, richest, smartest person on the planet. But I will tell you this: I feel like I am spoiled by a good Father, who loves me and gives me good gifts. He placed me in a church family with talented people and in a world that is covered in His fingerprints. Now my aim is not to be the greatest or to have the most but to be a good steward, investing all He has given me into His work. And He keeps entrusting me with more!

God Is Diverse

Jesus replied: "A certain man was preparing a great banquet and invited many guests. At the time of the banquet he sent his servant to tell those who had been invited, 'Come, for everything is now ready.' But they all alike began to make excuses."

—Luke 14:16–18a

In Luke 14, Jesus told a parable about a master who was throwing a banquet. When everything was ready for his guests, all he got was excuses. After hearing the excuses of those who were too busy, the host of the banquet told his servant, "Go out to the highways and hedges and compel people to come in, that my house may be filled" (Luke 14:23 ESV). God did not make His world or your world for your comfort and self-pleasure. He did not just want the house empty, swept, and put in order. He wanted it filled with all kinds of life.

When sin entered the world, man wanted to be the center. The harmony that existed between humanity and God was broken, and division came among people and creation. We forget that God is the One holding it all together. Each part of His creation has something to contribute, and it reflects Him best when everything and everyone comes together. Man does not delight in diversity but can love and unite with only that which is like him.

I believe that united diversity is a reflection of a God-centered universe. When people live in and enjoy diversity, there is a great reflection of God as the center. This is far different from the world in which we live. For example, throughout the Bible, marriage was for intimacy, fruitfulness, and filling the earth with life, but now—although people want all the benefits of marriage—there is a belief that having babies is adding an undesirable burden. The dream in our culture is to have huge houses with tons of rooms and only two people living in them. Filling homes with babies is viewed as too much work and sacrifice. But God doesn't create spaces to be empty. The spaces God gives us need to be filled.

Filled with Every Kind

I want to highlight what Genesis 1:20 says: "Let the skies be filled with birds *of every kind*" (NLT, emphasis added). Part of God's creativity in creation involved diversity. He didn't just create one species that had everything in common. He created a multitude of species, and He even made diversity flourish within the same species. God didn't just make one bird; He made birds of every kind. There was no limit to His creativity, and in the very beginning, He saw how all of that diversity would work together for a unified purpose.

Pastorally, I would say that many of us operate in fear and focus on only one kind of thing when we hear that God wants to fill our world. We probably would love for Him to fill our lives with wealth, possessions, power, and so on, but I don't think that's solely what Jesus meant when He said that He came to give us a full life (John 10:10). We are not meant to walk this road alone, nor can we fully reflect the glory of God in isolation. Therefore, God fills our lives with community.

The fifth and sixth days of creation show us that God created us to live in community and be filled. God said, "It is not good for the man to be alone" (Genesis 2:18). This shows a break in God's pattern of calling His creation good. Up to this point, God said that everything He made was good. But when He saw that the man did not have a suitable companion, it was the first time He said that something was *not* good.

In truth, we need each other—not just for our own benefit, but also to be a full reflection of the Trinitarian God of the Bible in the world. He is God in community! He is three Persons in one!

We cannot reflect Him if we are living in isolation, disconnected from diverse community.

God never intended for us to exist merely as individuals. Sometimes I think that the American gospel is too individualistic, with an "it's just me and God" mindset rather than a communal approach. God hasn't just called us into a new relationship with Him; He has called us into a new, diverse humanity. This new humanity, the church, is to be a reflection of all nations, tribes, and tongues.

As God's good creation, we need each other. This need for community is twofold. First, we need each other because we need help. Second, we need each other because our unity reflects our God to the world. Jesus said, "By this everyone will know that you are my disciples, if you love one another" (John 13:35). As His image bearers, we need each other!

God has worked and created in you, and He desires for you to live fully as the newly created you. You must know the good news that God loves the world! He is not just making you, as an individual, a new creation; He is making a new *humanity*. In Christ, He is making all things new. You can't walk into God's new creation if you're thinking that you can do it alone.

I saw the Holy City, the new Jerusalem, coming down out of heaven from God, prepared as a bride beautifully dressed for her husband....

One of the seven angels who had the seven bowls full of the seven last plagues came and said to me, "Come, I will show you the bride, the wife of the Lamb." And he carried me away in the Spirit to a mountain great and high, and showed me the Holy City, Jerusalem, coming down out of heaven from God.

—Revelation 21:2, 9–10

Revelation shows a picture of the new Jerusalem, where the church—in all of its diversity—is *collectively* the bride of Christ. Our unity here and now is a picture of what is to come.

This process of creating a new humanity is God's pattern throughout His story. Adam was the figurehead of humanity. When God did His works of redemption, He chose a figurehead who represented a family. He chose Noah, who, with his family, became a new humanity. He chose Abraham and the children of Israel as His covenant people, who were to be the new humanity and show the world a different, better way. He sent Jesus to be the head of the church, His new humanity. As God's family and covenant people, we are called to be a new humanity.

You need to find a church community that becomes your family, not just a church to attend. When we close ourselves off from society, we are not acting in the gifting of who God has created us to be and are not investing in the fellowship and community of others whom God has called us to serve.

If we are to look at what Jesus has done in us to form a new humanity and see what all those around us bring to our lives, then we need diversity. We can't have a one-dimensional focus. If we're going to walk in this new creation, we have to do it together. If we are to be filled with the life of God's grace, we need a diverse community.

People who think that they are already filled make excuses because they think they have enough. But on our own, we are nothing. We don't have enough. We need Christ creating in us.

God filled the earth, and He certainly can fill you. But He doesn't stop with just you, as an individual. His vision is much bigger than that. He sees a diverse, unified church filling the earth with His glory.

Step Five of God's Creative Process: Diversity in Unity

So in Christ Jesus you are all children of God through faith, for all of you who were baptized into Christ have clothed yourselves with Christ. There is neither Jew nor Gentile, neither slave nor free, nor is there male and female, for you are all one in Christ Jesus.
—Galatians 3:26–28

In truth, Jesus brings us together because together we reflect the glory of God. My professor Dr. Michael Goheen once said something in class that impacted my life immensely. He was giving a teaching on what the apostles where speaking into when they wrote the Epistles. He said one line in passing that stopped me in my tracks: "One of the burning questions of the whole New Testament is the reconciliation of Jew and gentile."

This speaks to the type of community the apostles were fighting for. If you read Romans, Ephesians, and Corinthians, you will see that the apostles were pressing into how the church should live. This new creation would have to be filled with a community of all kinds: Jew and Greek, male and female, rich and poor. All were one in Christ while still having their differences.

In the beginning, after the creation of the world, sin caused major separation between humanity and God and among all of creation, including races, ethnicities, classes, and ages. However, what Jesus did through His sacrifice on the cross has brought everything back together. In creation, God filled our lives with all kinds of life. He is continuing this same pattern in His new creation, bringing all things back together, reconciling all things in Himself (2 Corinthians 5:17–21).

> *For the creation waits in eager expectation for the children of God to be revealed. For the creation was subjected to frustration, not by its own choice, but by the will of the one who subjected it, in hope that the creation itself will be liberated from its bondage to decay and brought into the freedom and glory of the children of God.*
> —**Romans 8:19–21**

A full life is filled with various relationships. We see the beautiful reality of how, together, we reflect the glory of God. I love how a church family shows this reflection. I love my church, and I have had the joy of being in a family filled with all kinds of people from all ethnicities, ages, classes, and genders. We are greatly blessed because of it.

Still, life is hard, community is hard, and conversation is hard because we are a diverse people with diverse personalities and interests. Many people look at diversity and talk about how hard that kind of life is, how they want a comfortable church where everyone is just like them. But that isn't reality. If we don't unite with others, our lives won't be full, and we won't experience the entire glory of God. We need the various kinds of life with which God has filled our community. I think the separation of the church into single images we have carved out of our one-dimensional communities looks more like idolatry than like God's filled world.

Division destroys human relationships and is, unfortunately, flourishing in the world. Sin took what God made one and separated it. All of creation is groaning because of this separation.

This has especially affected relationships. People continue to segregate and fight. There is plenty of evidence of this in the world, but what concerns me most is division in the church.

Scripture continues to show us that the gospel is a grand declaration that all things, which have been separated because of sin, are being made one again in Jesus. The main argument in the book of Ephesians is that all people are coming together into one because of the work of Christ. People of all races and socioeconomic classes, men and women, are one in Christ. We need to commit to living in unity with our families no matter how different other members are from us. We cannot afford to be divided by race, ethnicity, social class, or gender. That is not and was never God's vision for His church.

And they sang a new song, saying: "You are worthy to take the scroll and to open its seals, because you were slain, and with your blood you purchased for God persons from every tribe and language and people and nation."

—Revelation 5:9

The church should look like a new humanity that reflects the God of diversity. I am saddened by all the divisions in the church, and I pray that you would be part of a community that is not about everyone being the same, but instead values all those created in God's image and likeness.

In my local church, we strive to embody this diversity. We aren't perfect, but it is our aim to reflect our diverse God to this world. I get to co-pastor our church with my dear friend, Wayne Wynter, an African American who comes from the streets of New York, and I am a white guy from the suburbs of California. We are part of a diverse leadership team made up of all types of people: men and women, rich and poor, diverse ethnicities. We are in the inner city, worshipping and doing life among the poor. In our congregation, it is not uncommon to have someone without a home worshipping right next to a wealthy business leader. This community endeavors to show love and inclusion without partiality.

> *But the wisdom that comes from heaven is first of all pure; then peace-loving, considerate, submissive, full of mercy and good fruit, impartial and sincere.*
>
> **—James 3:17**

> *For God shows no partiality.*
>
> **—Romans 2:11** *(ESV)*

I know that we are far from a perfect church, but we have been intentional about living in unity within diversity because we believe that the gospel is about reconciliation (2 Corinthians 5:18).

On a broader scale, I get to lead in a diverse multi-congregational church, Redemption Church Arizona, with nine congregations. Each congregation is different, with its own location, leaders, budget, building, and gifts, yet they all serve Arizona together. There is unity in diversity across churches. They are all different, but they are all unified in their purpose. I also sit on an executive team in a multi-denominational, multi-ethnic, multi-everything network called Surge Network. We are striving to serve Arizona and live in unity across churches from different traditions.

Just as a body, though one, has many parts, but all its many parts form one body, so it is with Christ. For we were all baptized by one Spirit so as to form one body—whether Jews or Gentiles, slave or free—and we were all given the one Spirit to drink. Even so the body is not made up of one part but of many.

Now if the foot should say, "Because I am not a hand, I do not belong to the body," it would not for that reason stop being part of the body. And if the ear should say, "Because I am not an eye, I do not belong to the body," it would not for that reason stop being part of the body. If the whole body were an eye, where would the sense of hearing be? If the whole body were an ear, where would the sense of smell be? But in fact God has placed the parts in the body, every one of them, just as he wanted them to be. If they were all one part, where would the body be? As it is, there are many parts, but one body. . . .

Now you are the body of Christ, and each one of you is a part of it.
—1 Corinthians 12:12–20, 27

My whole life has been changed countless times because of doing life together with men and women from all walks, skin colors, cultures, and backgrounds. My church is not just about *doing* service; it's about *being* the family of God. I love them in their messes, and they love me in mine, and we are thankful for the covenant we have with God and each other.

I encourage you not just to be a church attender, but to be deeply part of the new, diverse humanity with Jesus at the head. Love your brothers and sisters. Choose a community that does not look just like you, a community where you can learn from and serve all of God's people.

It may seem like I think it is easy, but I know that it's not. I know that walking in diverse community is costly—so costly that Jesus gave His life for it. I know this is miraculous and a work of the Spirit, but it is worth fighting for. For your spiritual growth, maturity, and mission, you need to pray and commit to living in covenant community.

Chapter Five Prompts

*Unity and diversity are beautiful
reflections of a God-centered world.*

Meditate on these Scripture verses: Genesis 1:20–25; Luke 14:15–24; Revelation 7:9.

Ponder:

  ∗ God doesn't create space to leave it empty.

  ∗ When you remove the diversity of how God created the world, you can easily enter into idolatry of created things.

  ∗ Think about the mystery of the Trinity: three distinct persons—Father, Son, and Holy Spirit—as one. Journal or draw your thoughts.

_____
_____
_____
_____
_____
_____
_____
_____
_____
_____
_____
_____
_____

Questions: How much diversity (of race, culture, age, gender, economic status, etc.) do you have in your relationships? What have you learned about God and how have you grown closer to Him because of these diverse relationships?

_____
_____
_____
_____
_____
_____
_____
_____
_____
_____
_____
_____

Prayer: Think of the beautiful diversity of God's creation. Thank Him for the ways He reveals Himself through the variety of the created world, including the variety of people and personalities that make up His body in the church. Write out a prayer of gratitude.

_____

_____

_____

_____

_____

_____

_____

_____

_____

_____

_____

_____

Activity: Intentionally spend time with a new acquaintance who is different from you. Share a meal together and listen to this person's story. Ask if you may pray for or with the person. Snap a picture, print it out, and place it in your journal or somewhere you will see it and be reminded to pray for your new friend. Think of three other people with whom you could begin to foster a relationship that would add diversity to your life. Pray about practical ways you could get to know them and be a blessing to them.

Chapter Five | *Thoughts and Drawings*

Let There Be Rest

Then God said, "Let us make mankind in our image, in our likeness, so that they may rule over the fish in the sea and the birds in the sky, over the livestock and all the wild animals, and over all the creatures that move along the ground."

—Genesis 1:26

By the seventh day God had finished the work he had been doing; so on the seventh day he rested from all his work. Then God blessed the seventh day and made it holy, because on it he rested from all the work of creating that he had done.

—Genesis 2:2

As we continue this idea of building relationships in community, we eventually come to the concept of *why* we are building these relationships. What is the purpose behind them? For each person, that purpose varies. For God, the purpose is clear. In every relationship, we bear the image of God.

As we go deeper into why God created us and put us here on the earth, we uncover our true purpose in life that fits exactly what God has called us to do. I think that people are looking for at least four things: identity, purpose, provision, and rest. Not surprisingly, these four things are completely wrapped up in who God is and whom He created. We are looking for these things because they are part of God's original design for us.

"Let Us Make Man in Our Own Image"

Because we are created in the image of God, we can know our true identity! God valued us above all His creation. We can see this when God got hands-on with His image bearers. Mankind has been touched by its Creator and given a special role in creation.

It is not the dirt that makes us unique; it is the breath God breathed into our lungs after He shaped us with His own hands. On the sixth day of creation, God broke the pattern of how He created all other things. On this day, God did something unique and special. Instead of saying, "Let there be…," He said, "Let us make…." The Trinity was speaking to one another. Then God reached into the dust, and He created and formed man.

In chapter 2 of Genesis, Scripture goes into more detail about the sixth day of creation. Genesis 2:7 expounds, "Then the Lord God formed a man from the dust of the ground and breathed into his nostrils the breath of life, and the man became a living being."

In this verse, the Hebrew word translated as "the breath," *něshamah*, means breath *or* spirit.[3] God's Spirit fills us and gives us life. We are created with value because we are created in the image of God, with His breath in our lungs.

You are an image bearer of God and a child of God. You were created with value before you ever accomplished anything. I am not sure where you are in your life, but if you can see that you are in Christ and He is in you, I pray that you will confess what is true about you. Say, "I am an image bearer of God." You don't have to look in other places to find your identity. Your true identity is found only in God.

A Part to Play in God's Work

For we are God's handiwork, created in Christ Jesus to do good works, which God prepared in advance for us to do.
—Ephesians 2:10

God made His calling for His people in the world very clear in Genesis 1. He gave them dominion and called them to fill the earth. Our purpose in God's world is assigned to us by God. Sin leads us to chase our purpose outside of our Creator. God has "fearfully and wonderfully made" you (Psalm 139:14) and has a role for you to play in the world.

Stop chasing what you can receive only from following Jesus and His work in the world. Jesus told His disciples to follow Him, and He would make them what they were meant to be. He said, "Follow me, and I will *make* you fishers of men" (Matthew 4:19 ESV, emphasis added). He will make you into what He has purposed you to be.

Many Christians are exhausted from chasing their purpose, striving to reach it in their own efforts. But if you follow Jesus, staying close to Him, God will shape you and form you while you are on mission with Him. He will use your unique gifts to glorify Himself and bless the world.

No matter what your situation is right now, I encourage you to trust and state out loud that God has a role for you. Say, "I have a part to play in God's work in His world." My prayer is that as you trust Him, worship Him with what you have, and steward all He has given you, you will see that God is using you as an integral part of His story.

All You Need

And my God will meet all your needs according to the riches of his glory in Christ Jesus.

—Philippians 4:19

It is hard to believe that we have all we need, because many of us are looking to God's creation for fulfillment. In Genesis 1, God provided all that mankind needed according to His riches in glory. But when all you see is lack and longing around you, it is hard to tell Christ, "I have all I need."

I'm sure that there are times when you wonder how God will take care of you and provide for what He has called you to do. I encourage you to think back on the

times when He provided for your needs. If you are in Him

and He is in you, then you have a Provider who knows what you need in order to do the work He has called you to do. Confess this truth, even if it is hard: "I have all I need." When you do not live in fear, you will take what God has given you and, with thankfulness, will steward and invest the gifts He has put in your hands rather than thinking that you need more.

God Does Not Stop Creating in You

Thus the heavens and the earth were completed in all their vast array. By the seventh day God had finished the work he had been doing; so on the seventh day he rested from all his work. Then God blessed the seventh day and made it holy, because on it he rested from all the work of creating that he had done.

—Genesis 2:1–3

You were created for *fulfillment.* You were created for *value.* You were created for *meaning* before the world ever began, and you are wholly precious in God's eyes. You are the likeness of Christ, and He does not stop creating in you. However, when God finished the work, He rested because His work was done.

When we think of rest, we think of plopping on the couch after a hard day's work and shutting down. But just because God rested doesn't mean that He stopped all activity in a couch-potato kind of way. He blessed His creation, and He sanctified the day. He made a day of rest to enjoy His creation. Rest is enjoying all that has been done.

God made this day and embedded the Sabbath in all of time. He wanted His people to have this day to enjoy and remember. When we take a day specifically set aside to worship and remember God, we are reminded of who He is and who we are, and we can enjoy all God has given us. This act of rest and remembrance takes our focus away from thinking that we never have enough.

Having a weekly Sabbath embedded into your life provides the opportunity to re-center your focus on the finished work of Jesus as you approach the week ahead. In this way, you end up working *from* the Sabbath rather than living *for* the weekend.

God continued this pattern of rest at every significant new-creation juncture. The children of Israel were chosen and made a separate people before God brought them out of Egypt, and God's protection and grace were on them as they followed Him into the desert. They were to know God's commands and obey them. They were provided with luminaries in all seasons—prophets, judges, and kings—to remind them, and He blessed them and filled them. He called them to know who they were as His chosen people, and He wanted to bring them into rest in the promised land.

Enter God's Rest

There remains, then, a Sabbath-rest for the people of God; for anyone who enters God's rest also rests from their works, just as God did from his. Let us, therefore, make every effort to enter that rest, so that no one will perish by following their example of disobedience.
—Hebrews 4:9–11

Hebrews 3 centers on the faithfulness of Jesus, our High Priest. The faithfulness of Jesus motivates our faith in the gospel, which allows us to enter God's rest. Hebrews 4 shows us that the Israelites did not enter into that rest because they did not believe the Word or the promise. Hebrews 4 borrows language from creation and the promised rest of the children of Israel to show that just because God provided this rest does not mean we will enter into it.

Up until the end of Hebrews 4:3, when the writer spoke of rest, he spoke of rest in the land. In verse 4, he spoke of rest on the Sabbath, and in verse 5, he linked the two kinds of rest. For the writer of Hebrews, these two concepts merged and were fulfilled in Jesus. Rest was a day or a place, but now true rest is in the finished work of Jesus. The work is done, and He is our place of rest.

> *You make known to me the path of life; in your presence there is fullness of joy; at your right hand are pleasures forevermore.*
> —**Psalm 16:11** *(ESV)*

One of the hardest things we can do is learn to enjoy and rest in God. We tend to think that the work is not finished and we have much more to do.

Jesus came and was the light. He lived among chaos and darkness, trusted His Father completely, remained faithful, finished the work on the cross, and entered into His rest, seated at God's right hand (Colossians 3:1). The gospel proclamation is that Jesus finished the work! Now we can rest from our constant striving and trying to earn something that is already ours, and we can find something that we already have in Christ.

Jesus finished the work, and Hebrews warns us to be careful to enter into that rest. We should be actively seeking to enter into that rest, which was provided for us by the finished work of Jesus. Jesus has given us the perfect identity from the very beginning of creation.

God made him who had no sin to be sin for us, so that in him we might become the righteousness of God.

—*2 Corinthians 5:21*

Because of our union with Christ, we no longer have to strive to find identity, purpose, provision, or rest. The new covenant we have with Him makes us whole and complete before God. Now we do not strive for rest; we live and work from a place of rest. Now we don't look for identity; we are in Him. We don't chase purpose. God declares purpose over us, and, by His power, we live it. We don't work for provision; we have a Father who provides. This is a new way of living. We are living in Christ, and Christ is living in us.

God Sustains You

Restore to me the joy of your salvation and grant me a willing spirit, to **sustain me**.

—*Psalm 51:12* (emphasis added)

Everything God has for us can be summed up in four categories: identity, purpose, provision, and rest. These categories capture all of life. *Identity* is who you are and comes in the form of your personality, desires, and goals. *Purpose* is what you are here to do and who you are created to be. *Provision* is what you do with whatever you have been given. *Rest* comes from confidence in who you are, what you were created for, and where you are going.

Let's look at our story about Hope. She didn't think that she would ever feel valued or loved because of what she'd experienced as a child, but God made her a new creation. Now she is married to a pastor, leads ministries, is a mother to five amazing children, and is growing in grace. Hope found hope in Christ. She found hope in how God values her as an individual. From there, Hope was able to forgive, learn, grow, and move forward in hope. Now she awaits the day when hope will be no more because her hope will be realized when she is at rest with Jesus for all eternity.

Of all these stories, none is more personal for me than the story of Hope because it is the story of my wife. I look at Dana (her real name) and everything she has overcome through the rest she found in Jesus, and I know that God is real.

What about the other stories? Where are these individuals now?

Carl struggled in his singleness and married his wife quickly. Over the years, I watched him struggle with unfulfillment after he was married. But God used his wife and kids as lights to show him what true fulfillment looks like. They have given him so much love and grace.

It has been a very bumpy journey, but God has been faithfully forming Carl into a man who is satisfied in Christ. Carl continues to follow Christ and has seen many addictions broken and new desires formed in his heart. God has a calling on his life! His story is not done being written; this is only the beginning. My greatest joy as a pastor is to watch God do powerful things in people's lives! Carl is a testimony of God's patient power.

Rosa didn't give up on her dream of being a psychologist. She learned how to integrate her desires into loving her family and meeting their needs. When her kids grew up and moved into what God called them to do, Rosa was prepared to move into the next stage God had for her.

Raising a family and caring for her husband while taking classes at night and online wasn't easy, but Rosa knew that's what God was calling her to do for that season in her life. Now, in this new season of her life, she has opened a small, full-time practice where she can completely enjoy what God has for her.

Kendrick continues working his back-breaking job during the day but is also involved in some music gigs on the weekend. In my eyes, he has become a fixture of what it looks like to be authentic and to care for people by using his gifts.

His music is professional, and he helps to produce and release music by other artists. His life is often challenging, but because he recognizes who God is and the purpose of God's work in the world, he can faithfully navigate through the journey on which God has him. He is talented, and I know that God is still forming him into all He has planned. The best part of this is that Kendrick isn't looking to music for his rest; he is learning to find true rest in Jesus every day.

Because of our human desire to do everything ourselves, we often have a hard time accepting the roles or jobs God gives us, so we don't look at work like we should. What would it be like to look at your vocation, your calling, and the ways you serve as part of God's work in you? Perhaps, like with Kendrick, Rosa, Carl, and Hope, it would give purpose to everything you do. No matter what job you have, it plays a huge role for you as an image bearer of God.

If God gave you the identity He wanted you to have from the time of creation, then certainly He has given you everything you need to sustain the work He has called you to do. He has provided for you in so many ways that if you simply listen and look, you'll be amazed at how He can use your passions and desires.

Once you fully recognize how you were created, how God has created in you and through you and for you, then you will be able to display rest. This comes from learning how to rest in God and have confidence in Him.

We often feel like we are lacking on many levels. What if you were willing to say, "I have been given all I need, and I can do whatever God has for me"? This mindset can change the way you view God's provision. You can be thankful no matter how much you have, knowing that it is all provided by God. God has built into His creation all you need to accomplish the work He has called you to do, and He will sustain you.

Step Six of God's Creative Process: God Comes to You

We are spending our lives pursuing value and rest in the God who created us and gave us life and purpose. We are in pursuit of rest. Scripture shows us that God came and walked with His people. I'm thinking of Adam and Eve, Noah, Elijah, Methuselah, Joseph, Paul, Peter, and John.

God enjoys us and wants a relationship with us—not just a working relationship, but a close, covenantal relationship. This life is not about climbing a ladder, working our way back to God. No, our God is the initiator. Our God is the One who comes looking for us. Though He is holy, He is not offended by our brokenness. He doesn't run and hide when He sees our sin. In Genesis 3, after Adam and Eve fell short of God's glory, God *went looking for them* (Genesis 3:9), and He continues this pattern throughout His story. He still goes looking for His children. You may feel like it's your job to climb your way to heavenly places, but you can rest in knowing that God comes to you.

> *Now the tax collectors and sinners were all gathering around to hear Jesus. But the Pharisees and the teachers of the law muttered, "This man welcomes sinners and eats with them."*
>
> *Then Jesus told them this parable: "Suppose one of you has a hundred sheep and loses one of them. Doesn't he leave the ninety-nine in the open country and go after the lost sheep until he finds it? And when he finds it, he joyfully puts it on his shoulders and goes home."*
> **—Luke 15:1–6a**

God wants you to operate this way, to operate in rest. You are not operating in rest if you are always striving, constantly unable to enjoy God and all He has given you. The risk of not being able to find rest lies in people who are not secure, who don't know who they are or what they have come to do. These people are unsatisfied with life.

God is still creating. Change is not often accomplished overnight. He has made you a new creation, but it's an ongoing process. I think that the most overwhelming reality about change is when you see how far you are from where you should be. You want perfection apart from the process, but that's not how God works. The beauty of the gospel is that we are made perfect in Christ, so we are not striving for perfection. We are in the hands of a perfect God, who has us in His process. When you surrender to God's purpose, you also need to surrender to His process and pattern.

Chapter Six Prompts

You will know your value only when you are living under the rule of God and not chasing your value in other places.

Meditate on these Scripture verses: Genesis 1:26–2:3; Psalm 139:14–15; Exodus 20:8.

Ponder:

* The image of God is not the dirt; it is His breath.

* You will know your purpose only when you are reflecting God in this world and stewarding, cultivating, and caring for what He has given you.

* Ponder the thought of God resting on the seventh day. Why did He rest? What does that show about God's character and the importance of rest? Write or draw a picture of your thoughts.

_____

_____

_____

_____

_____

_____

_____

_____

_____

_____

_____

_____

_____

Questions: When you hear that you are created in the image of God, how does that affect the way you view yourself? You are created with purpose. How can that change the way you live?

_____

_____

_____

_____

_____

_____

_____

_____

_____

_____

_____

Questions: God has given you everything you could ever need. In what ways are you serving Him with those gifts? Jesus has finished the work, and you don't have to earn your Father's approval. In what ways are you practicing the rest that you have in Him?

_____

_____

_____

_____

_____

_____

_____

_____

_____

_____

_____

_____

_____

Prayer: Like David in Psalm 139:14, thank God for creating you in such an amazing way! Write out a prayer thanking Him for His amazing re-creation, made possible through the finished work of Jesus.

_____

_____

_____

_____

_____

_____

_____

_____

_____

_____

_____

_____

Activity: To continue growing in what God has taught you through this study, write out a plan for how you will review and meditate on the things you have learned. Continue to write or draw insights in your journal regarding God's creation work in your life.

Chapter Six | *Thoughts and Drawings*

An Open Invitation

This book is certainly not the end of a journey, but a call for you to discover who you already are in Christ, to know your identity as His image bearer, and to rest in the finished work God has accomplished for you. This is the highest purpose you can ever have because God truly is the shining star in your new-creation story.

What humanity wants more than anything, what we think will make us happy when we get there, reveals much about our priorities and what we think will bring fulfillment. We often designate our fulfillment to a time and place in the future that we are never able to reach.

And yet, what you think you can't reach is indeed possible. Repent of making your dreams part of your creation instead of God's creation. When you cry out, "Create in me," your trust is in the Creator to do a glorious work in you in the pattern and order of His creative process. He will give a revelation of the work and life of Jesus. He will be your light and life.

God will help you to live in the space of His grace as you lean into and walk with Him throughout the new-creation process. He will lay a foundation of faith, making achievement possible through obeying and listening to Him.

Be patient as He walks you through different seasons of your life. He will give you His guiding light and lesser lights to point you back to Him. Remember that God is filling your life with all kinds of diversity and community. Jesus has done the work so you can be rooted in Christ as you live and breathe, resting completely satisfied and fulfilled in His grace as you serve Him and others.

When you see that you're living for God's glory and purpose, you're released into freedom because your life is from Him and for Him. You will never find your created purpose until you find the Creator's purpose. This truth will set you free and launch you into a life of trusting the Creator's process and pattern.

If we are honest, we'll admit that we don't mind change as long as it doesn't take too long to complete. It's like the old adage about ripping off the bandage quickly so that the pain is over almost before we even know it. But God graciously transforms us over a period of time. I can't map out that time frame for you, but I know that God is faithful to lead you out of bondage and separation, through the seasons of life, and into the promised rest. He who began a work in you will be faithful to complete it (Philippians 1:6).

Your rest does not come from thinking that you can earn God's favor or make yourself into what He created you to be and do. Your rest comes from trusting in Jesus, following Him through the seasons of life, and stewarding all He has given to you. Be confident that He will bring you into that promised day when all striving will cease. He will come and make all things new, and you will enjoy Him forever.

True joy and fulfillment happen once you realize that you are to find your sole purpose in the God who created you. When your eyes are open to see this truth, you will be able to find, enhance, and be content with who you are as a person. Each moment, hour, day, week, year, and decade will be a learning experience as God continues to reveal Himself to you, to grow you, and to create in you all that He envisions.

The way God primarily reveals Himself in Scripture is not as a powerful Master but as a comforting Father. He wants to be known by His covenant with His children. He does His work in you because He wants you to enjoy Him and be at rest with Him in loving covenant.

Though this book seems open-ended, it is actually an open invitation into rest and work with your Father. You have the opportunity to spend all eternity enjoying Him. Instead of giving you answers or advice in this book, I joyfully proclaim what is better—union with Jesus! Walk with Him, depend on Him, listen to Him, follow Him, and in it all, enjoy Him. In Him alone will you find fulfilling purpose and true rest. It is here that you will find yourself in the best place: in the hands of the One who created the whole world and continues to create in you.

About the Author

Aaron Dailey is a preacher, leader, and author who resides in Phoenix, Arizona. For the past two decades, he has pastored faithfully among central Phoenix's urban, working poor in the church he planted, alongside his wife and five children. He has a passion to cultivate a vibrant, healthy church family filled with incredible diversity, and he has seen it take shape at Redemption Church Alhambra, which is one congregation in the multi-congregational church Redemption Church Arizona, where he sits on the leadership team as an executive leader.

Aaron also enjoys serving as an executive leader for Surge Network, where he gets to coach, resource, and network with bivocational, inner-city church planters, pastors, and leaders. He also has the honor of working with movement leaders in the Southwest as a catalyst for City to City North America.

Aaron's heart is simply set on worshipping Jesus. He is creative and loves singing, storytelling, art, preaching, and doing life in multi-ethnic, poor, marginalized, and humble places. He deeply values relationships and loves to laugh and joke with the people that make up his community. Aaron's passions come to life when preaching the gospel of Jesus, sharing the message of His grace, walking with people as they grow in Christ, developing leaders, and creating churches that reflect the family-identity of God.

Notes

1   *Dictionary.com Unabridged*, "sanctification."
    https://www.dictionary.com/browse/sanctification?s=t.

2   Reiner, Rob, dir. *The Princess Bride*. Act III Communications,
    1987.

3   Strong, James. "H5397 – něshamah." *A Concise Dictionary
    of the Words in the Greek Testament and The Hebrew Bible*.
    Faithlife, 2019.

Made in the USA
Monee, IL
18 May 2021